ALSO BY ANTHONY E. WOLF

"It's not fair, Jeremy Spencer's parents let him stay up all night!"
A Guide to the Tougher Parts of Parenting

"Why did you have to get a divorce? And when can I get a hamster?"
A Guide to Parenting Through Divorce

Anthony E. Wolf, Ph.D.

FARRAR   STRAUS   GIROUX

NEW YORK

"Get out of my life, but first could you drive me and Cheryl to the mall?"

A PARENT'S GUIDE

TO THE NEW TEENAGER

Copyright © 1991 by Anthony E. Wolf, Ph.D.

All rights reserved

Distributed in Canada by Douglas & McIntyre Ltd.

Printed in the United States of America

First edition, 1991

29   31   33   35   36   34   32   30

Library of Congress Cataloging-in-Publication Data

Wolf, Anthony E.

Get out of my life, but first could you drive me and Cheryl to the .
mall? : a parent's guide to the new teenager / Anthony E. Wolf. —

1st ed.

p.   cm.

1. Parent and teenager—United States.   2. Adolescence.

I. Title.

HQ799.15.W65   1991   306.874—dc20   91-18261   CIP

To Mary Alice

Acknowledgments

This book was edited by Patty Bryan along with her husband, Mike Bryan. Patty reorganized much of the book and along with Mike did substantial rewriting. I am indebted to the Bryans for their skill and professionalism. They were also a pleasure to work with.

I would like to thank my editor, Elisabeth Dyssegaard, for her support and help in the writing of this book, and my agent, Joe Spieler, without whom this book would not exist.

I would like to thank Sue Kline for editing help, and Mary Wolf, Mary Hurtig, Marvin Gettelman, Ellen Schrecker, Barbara Wolf, Sandra Wolf, Liz Klock, Rich Romboletti, JoAnn Murphy, and especially my wife, Mary Alice, for reading parts of and offering suggestions about the manuscript.

Last, I would like to thank Sandi Douglas, whose time and ready availability for typing made my work so much easier.

Contents

Contents

Contents

Contents

Preface

This is a guide to adolescents—how to understand them, cope with them, and, to the extent that we can, direct their turbulent lives.

Teenagers of today have been raised in an era of far less harsh parenting practices. Their world may be complicated and scary; nonetheless, they feel more empowered than teenagers of previous generations. They are mouthier, less directly obedient, especially at home. This change in teenage behavior is real. It requires a similar change in teenage parenting.

This book differs from other parenting books in at least one crucial way. It does not offer a set of teenage parenting rules, though it does provide concrete suggestions on how to deal with a wide range of teenage issues. Rather, it explains why teenagers do what they do; it gives you the ability to translate teenage behavior into its true, often less complicated meaning. Armed with this new way of seeing, parents will not need to be told what to do. They can make their own decisions, based on their general good sense and personal child-rearing beliefs. An example:

"Cynthia, would you please take out the litter box?"
"Why are you always picking on me?"

If you understand the development issues embodied in this typical response, you can translate Cynthia's words:

"No, I'd rather not take out the litter box. I would prefer to get in a fight with you."

Knowing the teenager's underlying message, parents can respond as they wish. One option would be:

"Don't you dare talk to me like that."

However, despite the intended lesson of the parent's words—they really do not want to tolerate this kind of disrespect (which is a fine message)—their teenagers unfortunately will always interpret their response differently. They will hear:

"Yes, I will fight with you."

And that leads them to respond:

"I'll talk to you any way I want."

Which, translated, means:

"Good, now let's keep this fight going, and maybe you'll even forget about the litter box altogether."

Parents with a clearer understanding of their teenagers' behavior may choose alternatives to such a self-defeating response.

Throughout this book, I have tried to re-create the voices of teenagers and their parents. The quotes and conversations in the text are not from real people but from my head, a distillation of all that I have heard over the years in my practice and in my life. This will give you access to the real but never recorded discussions that take place in people's kitchens, in their heads, mumbled as they leave rooms, or screamed out in shopping malls. Their accuracy will be for you to judge. But I believe you will recognize, as recorded nowhere else, those scenes that are a part of your life with a teenager. If you do, you will hopefully be reassured. You are not doing anything wrong: everyone confronts the same kinds of problems with teenagers.

Much of this book is funny. That's because I think much that goes on between teenagers and their parents *is* funny—if we can step back far enough from our lives to view our daily travails for what they are, instead of as deadly serious issues.

Finally, if this book achieves its goal, you may notice a strange transformation in those scenes that used to drag you down. With a new understanding of your teenager's psychological development and state of mind, you may find that those scenes are never quite the same again. They look different, less desperate, more like the inevitable interaction between a normally developing teenager and a caring parent. You may also discover that, seeing differently, you act differently as well.

"Get out of
my life, but first
could you drive
me and Cheryl
to the mall?"

Introduction

"Clarissa, would you please take those dirty glasses into the kitchen?"

"Why? They're not mine."

"I don't care if they're not yours, Clarissa. You live in this house and I am asking you to take those glasses out into the kitchen."

"But they're not mine. I don't have to do it."

"Clarissa, you're asking for it."

"You're asking for it."

Forty years ago the above conversation would rarely have taken place, but it's common enough today. Teenagers have changed. This is not an illusion. Teenagers treat the adults in their lives in a manner that is less automatically obedient, much more fearless, and definitely more outspoken than that of previous generations.

Introduction

"I never would have talked to my parents the way that Melissa does to me. Never."
"What would have happened if you did?"
"I would have gotten a smack in the face."

True enough, but the harsher ways of dealing with children, especially physical punishment, are no longer viewed as acceptable. Many parents still treat their children harshly; many still hit them. But such punishment is far less acceptable than it once was, even to those who do it.

This *is* the era of "permissiveness." As a result, the most effective weapons have been taken out of a parent's arsenal. No more hard smacks across the face for disrespectful back talk. No more backside tanning when rooms are not picked up on demand. It's inevitable that without these harsher forms of enforcement, children's behavior has changed. This is just human nature. The new teenager does feel freer to do as he or she pleases, especially at home.

The Entitled Teenager

Teenagers of today possess a distinct sense of entitlement. They have their rights.

"Yeah. My parents are supposed to take care of me. And they're not allowed to hurt me. They're supposed to protect me. I suppose that I should act better to them than I do. But even if I act like a jerk, they're still supposed to love me. No matter what I do."

This is good. We want them to feel this way. We have empowered our children and they feel the power. Still, we did not think they would be so ungracious about it. Ours is a generation of uncertain parents. We witness our children's less restrained behavior, and we do not understand and we do not know what to do. *We* would not have behaved that way. In the face of their teenagers' insolence, parents feel frustrated, mad, and, above all, inadequate.

"What can I do? I yell at her. I ground her. I take away privileges. But none of it seems to change her attitude."

Nor do the teenagers benefit from their parents' frustration. They become victims of the classic adolescent paradox. While they demand freedom, and fight to attain it, they still need to feel their parents' strength. Teenagers battle to dismantle their parents' authority, but they can be undone if too successful. A much discussed statistic states that three times as many adolescents kill themselves today as did so thirty years ago. Unquestionably, the more that adolescents feel themselves to be truly on their own and without their parents' support, the more vulnerable they are.

Yet for the average as opposed to the seriously troubled teenager, I believe things are not nearly as bad as they may seem. The new teenager is *not* impossible to deal with. Parents must learn to adjust and to rely on a different kind of strength than their own parents used.

The New Parent

"I'll tell you what the problem is. Teenagers today don't have any respect for their parents."

This is true. Old-style respect is gone. We have entered a new era in child rearing. Perhaps the old way was both easier and more pleasant, but it is gone. Nostalgia is acceptable, but that style of parenting also had a flaw, in my opinion. It was based in part on establishing fear. Creating fear as an explicit child-raising practice has some bad consequences. It can breed anger and resentment. It can intimidate and cause the intimidated to lose confidence in themselves. Perhaps worst of all, it tells children that in the service of getting what one wants, fear and intimidation are necessary and acceptable in everyday life.

Teenagers today are not pliable, and they say what is on their mind—always. Yet for all their mouthiness, especially at home, it is not clear at all that as adults these teenagers will be "worse" than their parents, either less caring or less motivated. They may be more caring and more motivated. They may, in turn, be better parents.

Besides, it is possible to elicit respect from teenagers; it's just of a different kind than the old version. This new respect can only be based on the strength and confidence of parents. This kind of strength of *character*, really, is not as easy to come by as a strength based on the switch or the belt. More confidence is required to employ this strength. With few apparent weapons in their arsenal, parents must stand up to all that their teenagers may dish out, and still come out with their heads high, their confidence intact, their position as the parents and the bosses still acknowledged, if begrudgingly. It is not easy. But it is possible.

The first step is to accept a child's right to say what he or she has to say, no matter how stupid or unreasonable. You don't have to listen to all of it, you can leave whenever you want, but you respect their right to say it. Then you say what you have to say, you stand your ground and are not blown away by the inevitable response. This kind of parenting earns respect. It's the strength *not* to descend to teenagers' level of name-calling, when they would lose respect for you. It's the strength to walk away.

"Don't you dare talk to me that way, Eleanor. When are you going to learn a little respect? I don't know what's wrong with you. You are going to have to shape up."

Eleanor rolls her eyes.
"Don't you roll your eyes at me. Do you want a smack in the face?"
"Go ahead. Hit me. I dare you."

Eleanor knows that the time for *that* was over with years ago. Perhaps the greatest skill for a parent today is learning not to be hurt, truly understanding that what teenagers say and scream means nothing other than that they are teenagers and this is how teenagers today behave, understanding that what they say and what they do in no way diminishes who you are and what you do. Your teenage children cannot diminish you unless you allow them to.

"Yeah, well, easy to say. But in the real world how can we as parents have the strength to rise above the daily onslaught?"

You need confidence, and not confidence that you are always making the right decision—nobody can do that—or that you are always in control of the kid—nobody can even come close to doing *that*. Rather, you need the confidence that you are the right person for the job and that your efforts are definitely not in vain.

You must understand what you say does have an impact on your teenager, despite much evidence to the contrary. You must know that you need not be perfect, that you can make mistakes.

"You may not like what I am saying. You may disagree with my decisions. You may truly think that I am wrong. I may in fact *be* wrong. But I am your parent and the decisions that I make are in my judgment what I think is best. Whether you like it or not, you are stuck with me. That won't change, at least not for the next few years. And that is the way I want it."

There is pleasant irony to all this. If parents can hold up

through the teenage years, they may get all that they ever wanted at the end of the process: an adult child who genuinely likes and respects you and is comfortable with you; a person genuinely considerate of others and, amazingly, considerate of you; a grown child who now appreciates all that you have done for him or her.

"You were a great parent, even though I know that I really gave you a hard time."

I

Adolescence

1

What Is Adolescence?

"Clarissa was so sweet. She always used to give me these cute little cards with hearts or smiley faces on them. They would say 'I love you, Mommy.' She was a treasure. She really was. I used to call her 'Mommy's little treasure.' And helpful around the house? She would always ask if there was anything she could do. I just don't understand what happened. She changed. And now she abuses me. She's a monster."

"Reuben and I always had a special relationship. We were very close. When he got home from school, he couldn't wait to tell me about his day, and he always wanted to show me his school papers. He was so proud of them. Sometimes he would sit in my lap, he wasn't embarrassed about it, and we would just talk. It was really very wonderful. But then he changed. Now he hates me. He can't stand to be around me. I can't touch him. I've lost him. I feel so awful, so rejected."

What Is Adolescence?

Adolescence is unlike any other period in life. Above all, it is a time of transformation. It is not a single event, but a number of major changes coming within a relatively short period. These changes turn nice little children into intimidating adolescents.

There are distinct differences between how boys and girls go through this traumatic period of their lives. Not all adolescent boys and girls behave in the ways described throughout this book, but there is no question that certain patterns of behavior are characteristic of each sex. And there are very real reasons why these patterns exist.

When does the process start? There is no clear beginning. Girls generally mature earlier than boys, both physically and emotionally; often they have most of the characteristics of adolescence by age twelve. Boys, on average, mature about a year later. But whenever the change begins, it will often seem rather sudden: one day a child, the next, something quite different.

With boys, the change may begin that first day when he combs his hair before going to school. With girls, it seems to happen on an otherwise uneventful day—a day that occurs with inexplicable frequency during February of the seventh grade. That's the day when Clarissa comes home from school and is asked to do something that in the past she has done quite willingly, even enthusiastically. But on this day—the first day of her adolescence—she turns to her parents and snaps, "Why are you always asking me to do it? You've got hands, too, you know."

Physical Changes

What are the changes of adolescence? The most obvious ones are physical. The kids get *a lot* bigger—not gradually, as they have been doing all along, but suddenly. The girls mature before boys, of course, so that an eighth-grade class offers the humorous spectacle of huge women walking side by side with little kids.

The bodies don't simply grow. They change. Girls, for whom the changes are probably more significant, take on a whole new shape. Their hips widen and their breasts develop. Boys develop more muscle, grow hair in new places, and confront a very different-looking set of genitals. When this physical maturation is finished, boys and girls look at themselves and do not see the same person who was there not long before.

Adolescence is the start of true sexuality. Girls menstruate. Boys produce sperm. Most important of all, both sexes begin to have sexual feelings. Prior to adolescence, during the period referred to as "latency," they had such feelings, but for the most part these were underground. Preteens do have some interest in sex and can engage in sexual activity, but it really is a low priority:

"Hey, wanna see the new series of 'Gross-out Cards'? They have a lady with worms coming out of her eye sockets."
"Yeah. Lemme see."
"Hey, kid, wanna see a picture of a naked lady?"
"Yeah, sure. Is it okay if I look at her later?"

With the dawning of adolescence, the naked-lady pictures knock the "Gross-out Cards" into oblivion. The sexual feelings brought on by the biological changes of adolescence are unavoidable. Like it or not, here we are! And these feelings change *everything*. Suddenly the world has a whole new coloring. Previously a neutral canvas, it is now imbued with sexuality. And the way in which the new adolescent experiences it is changed forever.

Intellectual Changes

"Mom, Aunt Edith and Uncle Ralph are probably going to get a divorce, aren't they?"
"Where'd you hear that?"
"I didn't. I just can tell by the way you and Dad talk about them."

"Dad, Mrs. Williams is very insecure, isn't she?"
"What do you mean?"
"You know, the way she acts so phony all the time."

In addition to changes in sexuality, a less obvious but nonetheless very important change of adolescence is that thinking processes jump to a whole new level. Teenagers understand concepts and abstractions in a way they were not capable of before. They can participate in adult conversations (although they probably won't choose to). They can see the world through adult eyes (although they often refuse to). In short, the world of the adolescent is infinitely more complex than what he or she had known before.

The Major Change: Turning Away from Childhood

All kinds of changes, physical and intellectual, mark adolescence. But the hallmark of adolescence—the transformation that defines this period of life—is a *psychological* change. It is the adolescent mandate. A new and powerful voice rises inside of children. They must obey this voice and, in doing so, their lives change forever.

Simply put, the mandate tells the adolescent to turn away from childhood and childish feelings. Since childhood is marked by the domination by parents, it follows that adolescents must turn away from their parents.

Before adolescence children were . . . children, and they were free to act and feel as children. They could love their parents openly and depend on them. But with adolescence, a new force within dictates that teenagers must now experience themselves as independent, and able to exist on their own. No more can they feel close to or dependent upon their parents.

This mandate eliminates the wonderful security of childhood. Day-to-day living takes on a quality of desperation. The independent self of childhood, which had been content to develop a basic competence in such matters as tying shoes and riding a bicycle, and always with Mommy and Daddy as a safety net beneath it, now begins to assume for itself the full responsibility for survival. Life is no longer a game. It is for real. Yes, the world has become an exciting place, but in this new world adolescents feel much more exposed and therefore more vulnerable than ever before. Things can get scary, even terrifying, and perhaps overwhelming.

This turn toward independence, toward a world separate from family and home, has always been at the core of adolescence, today and a thousand years ago. It is an inevitable process. More than anything else, it is responsible for most of the behavior that constitutes adolescence.

The Wish Not to Grow Up

The course of preadolescent childhood is played out in the continuing struggle between the mandate to grow up and the wish not to. On the one hand is the "baby self" which desires only the nurturing it has enjoyed for years. All pleasure. No fuss.

"After a hard day at school let me unwind and fill up with good stuff. Let me watch television and eat Doritos. I definitely do *not* want to hang up my coat."

What Is Adolescence?

Parents see their children act immature, irresponsible, lazy, and demanding, because the home is the natural realm for expressing the dependent, babyish mode of functioning.

But there is the other self beginning to develop slowly—the independent, mature self. This self reaches out and seeks gratification from meaningful interaction with the world. It sets forth to accomplish something, to develop competence. It is willing to deal with stress, to take on responsibility. It is even willing to hang up coats—but only at school, or at Grandmother's house. It is usually on view only *away* from the home, unseen by parents.

Normal development pushes toward an ever-decreasing role for the baby self. Adolescence is no more than the first, most traumatic stage in this ongoing struggle, exacerbated by the new awareness of sexuality and the mandate to separate from parents, to avoid unacceptable feelings of dependence. Once people reach adolescence and, ultimately, adulthood, most have resolved this conflict by choosing a life of growth and separation. This "decision" is what we label maturity. This is what's supposed to happen. Ultimately, they can even act nice toward their parents. But not during adolescence! Then, they very much remain children when they are home. And often, rather nasty children. This is a crucial point: operating in the baby-self mode is a way *not* to separate from the parents.

Some children seem able to move off to function independently more easily than others. Their trials of adolescence will be relatively smooth for all concerned. Other children, although unaware of their choice, remain far more eager to seek the bliss of unseparated babyhood and avoid the hassles of dealing effectively with the world around them. Some children need to cling, often provoking endless and senseless battles. Children who are not so good at functioning on their own will probably have a tougher adolescence than their peers.

Margaret and the Stairs

During childhood the two selves exist side by side, switching back and forth. When my daughter Margaret was not yet two years old, she would sit at the bottom of the stairs in our house and cry for twenty or thirty minutes. This happened almost every day for at least two months. That is a lot of crying.

Margaret's room was on the second floor, and she had already learned to go up and down the stairs by herself. The crying was her means of telling us she wanted to be carried up to her room. Sometimes—when she felt like it—she would go up the stairs by herself. At those times she actually liked the climb. But, for whatever reason, Margaret chose this issue on which to take a stand. And she devoted an enormous amount of time and energy to trying to make her mother and me carry her up the stairs.

Why? What was so important that day after day Margaret would make such a scene, and stay with it for so long?

Margaret was confronting a big issue. During the first part of her life, once she began to interact with her world, she had been Queen of the Universe. What she wanted us, her parents, to do, we did. Her will was our will. There was no separation. But then, to her delight but also to her horror, Margaret discovered that this did not have to be the case.

She had already tried the "no" experiment and discovered its results. A parent says, "Come here," and a child says, "No." The child then watches her own body to see whom it will obey. To her delight it always obeys her. But up until a child's first open defiance of her parents, she has no way of knowing who is in charge of her body.

The experiment has a second part. That is what Margaret was fighting for on the stairs.

"It's okay, sort of, that I'm in charge of me. But I certainly don't want to give up being in charge of you, Mommy and Daddy. If it is true that we are totally separate and have separate wills, then it means that I am actually on my own and that is not so good. For then I am alone and very little. I will have to do everything for myself. I will have to learn how to survive. And I do not like any of that. I prefer the old way."

Margaret was fighting to remain the absolute ruler of the universe—without any obligations or responsibilities. Who wouldn't?

The Bliss of the Baby Self

The baby self does not die easily. In fact, it lives on somewhere in all of us. It desires not just to rule the world but also to move back in time to the absolute bliss of babyhood, wrapped in Mother's arms, forever.

It is the baby self which, above all, is responsible for most of the day-to-day problems that parents have with their children and teenagers. Although adolescents reject the child in themselves, it remains. And though teenagers refuse to accept that they are in any way childish, they all act in a childish manner. The mandate of adolescence cannot dismiss the child. It only decrees that the baby self is no longer welcome. With their parents, adolescents have made their earliest and most powerful attachment. We touch within them a place that no one else can, a place of deepest love. Since our connection with them is the strongest, it is the most difficult to break.

The alternation between these two distinctly different selves, one mature, one babylike, is not only bewildering to parents. It can also drive us crazy. It's normal and healthy but it's not much fun.

A teenage version of "Margaret and the Stairs" would be this scene between Vanessa and her mother:

"Mom, can I go with Beth Anne and Kimberly to the mall after supper?"

"No, dear, you know you're not allowed out on school nights."

"But, Mom, please. I'll be home by nine-thirty. You know that's when the mall closes."

"No, Vanessa. We don't want you out on school nights."

"Mom, you're not being fair. You let Stephen do all kinds of stuff. Just because he's a boy."

"Stephen is older and, besides, that has nothing to do with it. I said no and that's final."

"I hate you. You never let me do anything. Why? Why can't I go?"

"Vanessa, you are starting to make me angry."

"You're getting angry? I'm the one who's not allowed to go to the mall. Why, Mom? You just like ruining my life."

The confrontation continues. Vanessa ends up in tears and storms off to her room, where she sulks for the rest of the evening. Her mother also remains in a bad mood.

This was not the first time that there had been such a scene, nor would it be the last. From previous experience, Vanessa knew full well what her mother's response to her request would be. Not only that, she knew the scene would end exactly as it did. Parents who have endured such scenes remember distinctly feeling that their child was after something, something more than just getting them to change their mind. From Vanessa's mother's standpoint, Vanessa seemed to be after a smack in the face. If not that, what did she want?

Why couldn't Vanessa accept "No," especially after a couple of attempts to change her mother's mind hadn't worked?

Vanessa was being asked to accept a loss. And this meant shifting over, however briefly, to her more adult, independent mode of functioning. She might have decided:

"Well, it's really no big deal. I would like to have gone out. I would have had fun. But I see them every day at school. It's no big loss. Anyway I can call Rachel and talk with her."

But picking up and moving on was not for Vanessa. On another day she might have accepted defeat. This time, especially because it was her mother—the object of her strongest, most babyish attachment—the baby inside of her dictated the scene. Separation, which would have ended the contact, was absolutely not what Vanessa wanted. Had she accepted the "No," her involvement with her mother would have been brief, but she kept after her mother and a lengthy scene ensued. Instead of separation, Vanessa achieved just the opposite, just what she wanted. She got passionate involvement over an extended period of time, even if it was in the form of yelling, crying, and sulking.

Not only can the baby inside of teenagers control their behavior. It can achieve this without their knowledge. Teenagers have an infinite capacity for self-deception.

"Me? No. My mom's the baby. She's the one who isn't mature enough to change her mind. I'm just trying to get to be a little more independent. She's the one who needs to grow up."

This is actually how they think. Acting like a baby? Even when they are yelling at parents who have locked themselves in a bathroom to escape the harangue, they are certainly not behaving childishly. No way.

A Self Without Conscience

This is a characteristic of the baby self: It does not look at itself. It does not judge itself. It is not bad. It is not good. It is not anything. It has no conscience.

"I'm not good-looking. I'm not ugly. I'm not a good person. I'm not a bad person. I'm not anything. When I'm home, I'm just me."

That's why adolescents can be so infuriatingly oblivious to their own behavior.

"How can you act this way?!"
"What way?"

They are not being intentionally difficult. In some kind of magical way, what they do at home exists in a sphere of its own. It has nothing to do with the adolescent's sense of self, with the kind of person he or she really is. They simply do not look at themselves. This is not something that the baby self does.

"Are you honest?"
"Yes."
"But you just lied to your parents."
"Yes, I know. I know I lied, and I know it doesn't make sense, but I am honest. Lying to my parents or my brother or sister is just not the same thing as lying to somebody outside the family."
"You mean lying to your parents is not dishonest?"
"Well, yes, it is, but I am not a dishonest person. I'm really not. I can't explain it. It just is that way."
"But you shouldn't lie to your parents, should you?"
"No, I guess not."
"You guess not?"

What Is Adolescence?

"I mean if it's bad, it's not very bad. It's just not the same as it is with other people."

Which Is the Real Self?

Which is the real self, the self who gives her parents nothing but grief and would seem to prefer death to helping around the house, or the self who assists her grandmother with household chores? The self who will not take out the trash at home—a routine chore for the previous three years—even when he trips over it, or the self who receives an award from his school booster club for his extraordinary efforts on "Clean Up the Town Day"? The self who looks like a slob when home, or the self who preens for over an hour to get ready for school?

Both selves are normal and necessary. Yet if parents want to know what their children are really like, if they want to get a sense of who their children will become as adults, the more accurate gauge is behavior *away from home*. The self that adolescents bring out to deal with the world is, in fact, a truer reflection of the real level of maturity they have achieved. At the very least, the behavior that parents see and endure at home is not necessarily the behavior their children exhibit elsewhere.

The Passion of Adolescence

Adolescence is unlike any other period in life. With it comes a special feeling, one that we never quite forget. During this time, attention and concern turn to the world outside, and away from family and home. Sexual feelings, newly emergent, increase the nature and intensity of that focus. The result is that the world becomes infused with incredible power and poignancy. The world is new—but this newness has a price.

As adolescents cut off dependence on home and parents, they feel much more on their own. And although not yet established in the big outside world, they can no longer use home as a fallback. Successes and failures in school and with friends seem absolutely crucial to continuing survival. *Everything* takes on a much more desperate quality. Because adolescents do not have much experience in life, they see only their day-to-day existence. They have no long-term perspective. None.

The world has become an exciting place, but in it they feel much more exposed, much more vulnerable than ever before. Moreover, their feelings have an undeniable power—a power that makes adolescence, however troubling, very, very special.

Where It's At

I can remember how, as a teenager, I would drive around in the car listening to a song on the radio that I liked and also feel pressure to turn to another station just in case it was playing another song I liked better. No matter how good the song I was hearing at the time, I feared missing out on something even more special.

Teenagers ride up and down the same stretch of road always on the lookout. They hang out in the parking lot of a restaurant talking in small groups or just waiting for something to happen. There is an expectancy in the air so real they can almost reach out and touch it.

"Hey, Jim, anything happening?"

"Naah. I just talked to Glenn and Kratzner and they said maybe there was going to be a party at some girl's house that I never heard of. I don't know. We'll probably hang around here, see if anything turns up. How about you?"

"I don't know. It's been pretty dead around here, except

there's this kid Ricky who's supposed to be looking for Larry Bronson 'cause he's pissed at him for something. But I don't know. We'll probably stay around here a little while and then maybe go over to Smiley's."

"Yeah, maybe we will too."

. Life is very powerful stuff for a teenager. It holds them continually in thrall. They cannot put the feeling into words, but they have a sense that something could happen out there that really would be what they're waiting for. It is both tantalizing and frustrating.

"What time is it?"
"I don't know. I think it's about twelve-thirty."
"I don't think anything's going to happen."
"Yeah. I'm probably just going to go home. I'll call you tomorrow."
"Yeah. See ya."

But adolescents would not want to go home until they were fairly sure that it was late enough. Late enough so that nothing would happen without them. *They would not want to chance missing it.*

What is the something that infuses the very air with unspoken potential? It is sexuality, certainly, but it is more. Prior to adolescence, children have loved their parents, perhaps a favorite pet, other attachments that are part of home. But with adolescence this capacity for passionate involvement and love, though it does not totally leave home, turns outward. However, it has little to attach to, especially in early adolescence. It lacks focus.

Only from adolescence onward can humans fall in love. In early adolescence such love is usually limited to powerful but transient crushes. Only later are deeper, more lasting love relationships formed. Mostly an adolescent's love is unfocused, diffuse. It lights up the whole world and produces the sense of inchoate longing that so characterizes early adolescence. Teenagers are, in effect, in love with the world, but their love is unrequited. They have great longing, but are never quite fulfilled.

Memories of Adolescence

A song from our past, a particular place, even just a smell can suddenly evoke in all of us the sense of another time and place. With this casting back in time comes a surge of feeling, poignant but fleeting, gone before we can catch hold of it. We picture clearly a piece of our adolescence, and we experience a deep longing. Yet the scenes that cause these feelings are often oddly unremarkable:

"I can picture a summer evening and me sitting with some friends at a picnic table outside a drive-in food place where we used to go. It wasn't like I always had such a good time. But I remember it as if it were something incredibly wonderful. I'm pretty sure it wasn't."

What we conjure in these moments, however fleetingly, is that special adolescent feeling of being in love with the world. It is a memory of the unique, unfocused passion of adolescence.

2

What They Do
and Why

The two main forces of adolescence are the onset of sexuality and the mandate that demands that teenagers turn away from childhood and parents. More than anything, these two forces shape adolescents. But their shapes can be strange, and they are usually very different for boys and girls. Though the underlying adolescent forces are similar for both sexes, what they produce is quite different.

Most teenagers do not act at all as they did when they were younger. Above all, how they act often does not seem to make sense.

Facing the Adolescent Mandate

Allergy to Parents

Allen was sitting on the couch watching television. His mother sat down next to him.

"What are you watching?"

Without a word Allen got up and left, went to his room, and turned on his stereo.

Mother: "I'm not good enough for him? He's repelled by me?"

Allen: "I can't help it. I'll be perfectly relaxed, and as soon as she walks into the room, I get totally tense and uncomfortable. It's not her fault. I can't explain it. I just don't like being near her, or Dad either."

Mother: "But it seems like he hates me. Like I disgust him or something. Why? What's his problem?"

It is the teenager's allergy to his parents. Even a parent's presence in the same room causes real discomfort. Worse yet, the parents might actually say, "Hello," or "How was school?" It is enough to make their teenagers' skin crawl. They cannot wait to get away, cannot wait for their parents to shut up. Being near their parents creates feelings of wanting to be near them, as always before, feelings of loving them and wanting their love. But these feelings are now totally repugnant. And because parents are the source of these unacceptable feelings, adolescents are repelled by their own parents. They still have feelings that pull them toward their parents, but these feelings are completely unacceptable to them.

"Just one time I want him for a full five minutes to sit in the room with me and we will talk about our day. I do not think this is an unreasonable request."

It is not. Parents are allowed to order their sons to stay in the room with them, even order them to talk. But the sons will squirm. Girls, of course, will not only squirm but also take intentional deep breaths, tap their feet, and roll their eyes.

Teenagers do not like to be touched by their parents for the same reasons that they do not like to be near their parents. It is still okay to give them hugs and kisses, but understand that they *will* squirm and try to get away.

The patterns of behavior caused by this allergy differ markedly for boys and girls. Boys, primarily because of their sexuality, choose the absenting method in dealing with Mom and Dad. They hide. Girls battle. Not all boys hide and not all girls fight, and not to the same degree, but there's no question that certain patterns of behavior are characteristic of the two sexes.

TEENAGE BOYS

Vanishing Experts

Once adolescence begins, teenage boys go to their room, close the door, turn on their stereo, and come out four years later. This scenario is not that much of an exaggeration. Some also spend a lot of time away from the house—a solution available to them because teenage boys are usually given more freedom than girls. In short, boys solve the problem of their need to separate from their parents by doing just that: physically separating. They become vanishing experts. They learn the trick of saying "yes" but doing "no." They agree to do what is asked of them, in order to avoid a fight, but then disappear before actually accomplishing the task in question.

"James, could you empty the dishwasher?"

"Sure, Dad, in a minute"—and then James is gone.

Above all, teenage boys become very private. They do not like to talk to their parents. In fact, they do not want their parents to know anything about what is going on in their life. The main reason is their sexuality. These feelings are an enormous part of a teenage boy's world. And this sexuality is something that he very much wants to keep separate from his parents. But it is also so much a part of him that the only way to keep it separate from them is to keep *himself* separate. The internal taboo against mixing sex and parents is so strong and the role of sexuality in a teenage boy's life is so pervasive that he is forced for the most part to shut his parents out of his life.

The Problem of Mommy

Boys are especially likely to avoid their mother. Most adolescent boys are attracted to women. For most boys there has already been one particular woman in their life whom they have loved deeply. Unfortunately, that woman is their mother. Hence, until they get their new and fairly amorphous sexuality firmly focused on females outside the home, their mother presents a problem. The possibility always exists that strong feelings in connection with a boy's mother might be tinged with sexuality and might therefore become *really* unacceptable. In fact, because everything with adolescent boys is so sexualized, strong feelings toward anybody are a problem until that sexuality is better focused.

Particularly troubling from the perspective of the mother is that her previously open, talkative, very huggable boy disappears absolutely and is replaced by a young man who seems to radiate an aloofness that, if anything, makes her feel scorned. The situation can create real problems. Hurt by her son's aloofness and feeling rejected, a mother may aggressively communicate her hurt to her son, which is the worst thing she can do.

"Why? Why do you act this way? You hate me, don't you? You actually hate me."

"Jesus Christ, Mom, will you get off my back. You don't know anything."

"There. You're doing it. You hate me."

"For Chrissake, Mom. Will you shut up!"
"Why? Why are you like this?"

Since strong emotional contact with his mother is especially upsetting to any teenage boy, he may in turn react strongly to his mother's anger at him. After all, he can't explain the facts of life to his mother because he doesn't really know what's going on himself. Can we imagine the following speech?. "It's not anything to do with you, Mom. It's my strong instinctive but normal reaction against my sexually tinged dependency needs. It won't be nearly as bad in a few years when I am more truly independent and when my sexuality is better focused on women outside the home." No, we can't imagine *or expect* this insight.

There is no solution for a mother beyond understanding that at this point in her son's life, he needs distance from her. She must accept his behavior, understand that its root is not dislike for her, and realize that in time it will change—and it will—when he becomes more truly independent—when he has his own sexuality better under control.

Fathers and Sons

What about fathers and sons? Fathers, too, are to be avoided, but the ban is not so stringent. The sexual taboo is not as major a distancing factor, but closeness and affection have to be carefully censored in order to avoid any sense of homosexuality. When fathers and sons are able to maintain contact it's usually in some sort of oblique relationship. They do not exactly relate to each other, but they can discuss topics of mutual interest, such as sports.

"Dad, did you see that Mark Jackson went one for eight from the field last night?"

"I know, I can't believe that the Knicks are still starting him. They traded the wrong guard when they got rid of Strickland."

But many boys cannot even tolerate that level of interaction.

Fight or Flight

Boys for the most part cannot battle verbally. They get little practice. They may engage in unsophisticated verbal sparring with their peers—"You're a faggot," "You're an asshole"—but past a certain point, the prevailing code says that you have to fight. Boys rarely develop the skills or the emotional capacity to stay with strong verbal scenes. The typical adolescent boy history includes few direct child-parent screaming matches.

If boys do become emotional with their parents, they tend to get very emotional. These occasional instances are often accompanied by a punched hole in the wall or a broken screen door flung open too violently as the boy storms out of the house. Boys avoid confrontation for the excellent reason that they can't handle it. They get too upset. It's either fight or flight, and at home they usually do the latter—which is good.

Boys who do battle regularly with their parents instead of isolating themselves can create serious problems. They are usually boys who, prior to their teenage years, remained strongly attached to their parents. In adolescence, their lack of separation takes the form of endless battling. With the addition of sexuality to their already strong feelings, the emotional scenes that such a boy provokes can become overwhelming for him. Serious—even scary—problems can result, and these will be the subject for future discussion. Fortunately, it is more normal for teenage boys to have as little to do with their parents as they can.

Slugs

One particularly irritating manifestation of this mandate in boys is a sort of absenting *even when present*. What happens is that teenage boys develop terminal lethargy. They seem to catch a lengthy case of sleeping sickness. They appear to do nothing. If the normal speed of human activity is thirty-three or forty-five rpm's, teenage boys seem to go at around six. Words like "wha?" and "hunh?" enter their vocabulary.

> *"Melvin, would you help me move the lawn furniture into the garage?"*
> *"Wha?"*

> *"Alexander, are these your soda cans in the family room?"*
> *"Hunh?"*

These boys have their new sexuality and they also have their future, which hangs like a disquieting cloud, ever threatening. "Do you really think you can make it on your own?" Boys do not like such thoughts. Such thoughts are disturbing. At home boys want peace and tranquillity. In this regard parents are a special problem because they are a constant potential source of aggravation.

"Didn't you say you had a history test tomorrow? Shouldn't you be studying?"

Boys seek to achieve a state of perfect passive pleasure. So do girls, but boys seem to do it more. Teenage boys seem to be particularly good at lying in bed, listening to music, watching TV, and doing nothing. They can get themselves into a state of total passivity, with no anxiety and with genuine comfort, screening out all unpleasant stimuli. But it must be worked at.

The teenage boy's pledge of behavior:

"I will do what I feel like doing, but, just as important, I will not do what I do not feel like doing. I will do my best to deal with my adolescence by devoting my life at home to having me feel as good as possible. And above all, I am going to avoid anything that is not going to make me feel good."

They may never achieve it but they try.

"Do you know what Mark did over spring vacation? He did nothing. You don't understand. I mean *nothing*."

TEENAGE GIRLS

The Never-Ending Battle

Girls deal with the psychological dilemma of adolescence differently from boys. Like boys, adolescent girls find it totally unacceptable to feel attached to, or dependent on, their parents. But girls do not withdraw. Unlike boys, they do not have to. Instead they fight. It is with girls, not boys, that parents experience the supreme disruption of adolescence. Sweet, cooperative daughters turn, often rather suddenly, into hysterical, shrieking monsters.

Girls solve the problem of living at home, and yet successfully combating their totally unacceptable feelings of love and dependence, by fighting everything.

"Whatever my parents say, I will shriek at, do the opposite of, disagree with. You say it, I'll yell at it. By doing this, I am obviously demonstrating, both to myself and to you, that I am not dependent and loving. How can I be anything other than independent of my parents if everything that they say to me I yell at? Also, whenever I think I can get away with it, I will sneak and lie."

"Sylvia actually told me that she wished that I had put her in a foster home when she was a baby, rather than grow up with me as her mother."

What They Do and Why

"My Jennifer swears at me all the time."
"Lydia told me to shut up. Can you imagine, just like that, she said to me, 'Shut up!' "

The major reason that teenage girls stay involved with their parents—however combatively—is that their new sexuality does not work against them. Sexuality, for most teenage girls, does not have the "in the air all the time waiting to be attached to anything" quality that it has for boys. It does not drive the wedge between child and parent.

In fact, because their sexuality is not such an issue in their relationship with their parents, some teenage girls can have a warm relationship with their father. That is, if the father is not too much put off by other characteristics of their adolescent behavior. Teenage girls can in fact have a warmer relationship with their father than with their mother. With almost all girls, the attachment to their mother is stronger than the one to their father, and therefore the adolescent mandate requires that much more negativism in order to deny that tie with the mother.

Teenage girls also argue far more than boys do as an outgrowth of earlier styles of fighting and relating to peers. Girls can talk about feelings. Girls can have very emotional, even nasty verbal fights with one another. They simply are better at and more comfortable with verbal interactions, even when they do get emotional. Therefore girls, having had the practice going into adolescence, are far better equipped than boys to deal with the emotional exchanges that characterize their relationships with their parents.

"I don't know why you think you're so great, Elaine. You know I've been to your house. You don't even have a washer and dryer. Your family has to go to the laundromat."

"I wouldn't talk, Janis. At least my father still lives at home. You say yours takes you out every weekend, but I'll bet he doesn't."

For teenage girls with histories of real dependency, who wrote uncounted numbers of "I love you, Mommy" notes, who could never do enough for Mommy, their dependent needs are still so strong, though suddenly unacceptable, that screaming and disagreeing may not be sufficient. These girls take the most drastic measures to reject their feelings. They battle the most violently, the most persistently. But sometimes even that is not enough. They run away—sometimes overnight, or longer. Often they gravitate toward those who are on the fringe, those who will accept them. They become the "bad girls"—often promiscuous, often the most daring. And it is they who are most at risk during their teenage years. The sad irony is that these girls who most violently reject the influence of home are actually the least self-confident and the most in need of guidance.

Even more ironic is the fact that these girls, once the storm of adolescence has abated, once they have established for themselves some sense that they are not so attached to their parents, come back home. They may return with many negative experiences behind them, perhaps even with a baby in tow, and they stay. Their adolescent independence was more show than substance. Now, only a few years removed from furious battling, they are back—perhaps never to separate totally again.

Battles Equal Contact

A battling teenage girl can certainly be more of a strain on parents than a disappearing teenage boy. Yet this battling is not as bad as it seems. Though they are disagreeing and criticizing, they are nonetheless staying in contact. By fighting, they maintain an ongoing relationship with their parents. They are using their parents for support. Boys more or less do not. They are unable to. (Perhaps this isolation contributes to the fact that boys' suicide rate is more than triple that of girls.) As a result, even though girls' adolescence is more tumultuous, at least at home, they also get more support. Girls can have it both ways. They can keep their dependency going via their continuing contact with their parents, however stormy, but they also get to feel that they are independent. Boys, because they isolate themselves and have nobody to lean on, are forced to deal with problems more on their own. They are perhaps more vulnerable to serious problems. If there is a consolation for adolescent boys, it is that some years later, in early adulthood, they seem to have an easier time leaving home *for good* than do many girls.

Parents Are to Be Taken for Granted

"*Mom, can you take me to the mall?*"
"*I really don't feel well, Elizabeth.*"
"*But I have to get a notebook.*"
"*You can go up to the corner store and get one there.*"
"*But they don't have the kind I like.*"
"*Don't you understand, Elizabeth? I'm really feeling badly.*"
"*Well, I need the notebook badly.*"

What are they, some kind of monsters? Don't they have any kind of consideration? Do they take us totally for granted? If we could get inside Elizabeth's head, we'd ask, "You really don't care that your mother is sick?" And she might answer, "No, it's her job to take me. She doesn't feel that sick. Besides, what am I supposed to do? I can't drive."

Worse yet, adolescents will be sensitive to hurt puppies, to starving children in distant countries, to a friend with a problem. But not to us, their parents. They do take us totally for granted.

"*What am I, a robot slave?*"
"*You're my parent.*"

"*Do you know how much time I spent driving you around last week?*"
"*What's that got to do with anything?*"

They just do not see it.

"*Mom, you're selfish.*"
"*I'm selfish? You're the most selfish, ungrateful child in the world.*"

Is she really a monster?

Not all teenagers are so inconsiderate. But many are. They do take their parents for granted, and nothing can change that. It is important to let teenagers know that they are being inconsiderate. Parents should refuse to be bullied—they always have the option of saying, "No." But like it or not, the teenagers' behavior, though obnoxious, is normal. Not only is it normal, but it does not mean in and of itself that they are selfish, inconsiderate people. It *is* a developmental stage, and it *does* change—even before the end of high school.

But most important, though their behavior is obnoxious, terrible, should be stamped out totally, it is not bad. Teenagers are children. It is precisely because their parents have been good parents, have given them the unconditional love and support that *should be* all children's due, that they can be so heedlessly obnoxious. They will openly admit to this a few years later.

"I don't know how you put up with me."

But not then. They simply do not see it. And though they are truly awful, and should be dealt with as such, they are still children.

Adults as Jerks

"Dad, why do you have to blow your nose like that? Nobody blows their nose and makes that much noise."

"Have you noticed that Miss Polnaggio has bad breath?"
"I know. Hasn't she ever heard of mouthwash?"

"Mom, how come you use that phony voice whenever you talk to Dad's parents?"

"Dad, if you know everything, how come you dropped out of college?"

It is very important for adolescents to begin viewing adults as flawed. Teenagers know that they themselves have flaws— lots of them—and they also know that they're expected to go out shortly into the adult world and survive. The natural thing to do is look for evidence that adults are human and flawed as well. If, instead, most adults are seen as perfect, or nearly so, the adolescent will doubt her own ability to make it once she becomes an adult. She knows her flaws are not going to disappear over the next couple of years.

Therefore it is particularly important for adolescents to view their parents as flawed. But for parents who have been accustomed to admiration from their children, this critical attention can be more than a little distressing.

"I don't have to take it. I am not going to stand for my own children criticizing me and even holding me up to ridicule. I am the parent, and I insist on remaining a figure of respect."

Lots of luck. It is normal and healthy for teenagers to prefer to see adults as fools. However, and ironically, teenagers also want to view adults as good and competent and worthy of respect. They do want to have adults to look up to—if they can find them. But now with their more adult and critical eyes, they see the flaws. What they ideally want to see, especially in their parents, is adults who are flawed but who are not thrown by their own flaws, and hence are still worthy of respect. Adults who act as if they know everything are hard for teenagers to stomach.

"I'm trying to get used to the idea that I'm going to be an adult but will still have lots of flaws. And here's some jerk acting like he's perfect, which nobody is. What an asshole!"

To get along with teenagers, parents need to accept that they themselves have flaws. Even better, adults should have a sense of humor about this state of affairs. Parents who do can become a model for their teenage children because teenagers also have trouble accepting their flaws.

Parents as an Embarrassment

When my son Nick was in high school, I would give him a ride to his bus stop if he was running late in the mornings. The bus stop, where maybe half a dozen kids were waiting, was around a sharp bend after a relatively straight stretch of road. Nick would always have me drop him off just around the bend from the bus stop. He did not want the other kids to see me dropping him off. What was his problem? He did not want the other kids to know he had parents? *They* probably had parents.

Rachel and her mother were shopping in a mall. Rachel's mother saw a couple of Rachel's friends ahead of them. Next thing Rachel had disappeared. She found her hiding behind a display in a toy store.

"Are they gone, Mom?"

Not only do teenagers see their parents as grossly flawed, they also find them outright embarrassing, especially if seen with them anywhere outside the home. The adolescent mandate says that teenagers must disinvest in parents and commit to the world separate from home. As a result, parents and the world out there—particularly friends—do not mix at all. Commingling between parents and friends is embarrassment beyond belief.

"He used to love going out with us to a restaurant or to the movies. We had such nice family outings. But now he flatly refuses to be seen with us in public."

"It's not that I want to be rude or anything but I feel like such a jerk when any of my friends see me with my parents."

"I can't stand it when my mom starts asking my friends questions when they come over to the house. Like she's trying to be friendly. I can't help it, but it drives me crazy. And one time she was driving me, Jenny, and Lynnette to the mall and we were singing this song and she joined in. I thought I would die."

In an ongoing joke that I used to have with my son I would forever threaten to sit down with him and his friends and talk as if I was "one of the guys."

"Hey, dudes, what's happening?"

It was Nick's greatest nightmare.

They Even Look Up to Some Adults, But Never Us

"Mom, don't buy any more potato chips, okay? Coach Thurgood says I should cut out eating junk food."

"Mom, you should be more like Yvette's mother. She really is great. Sometimes when I'm over at Yvette's I talk to her and she really understands stuff."

Many if not most teenagers find an adult whom they like, respect, and even listen to. Many adolescents do crave adult closeness and guidance, but since their parents can no longer be that chosen adult, they often find substitutes, usually a teacher, a counselor, a friend's parent, or even an aunt or uncle.

This behavior may be frustrating and even the source of a little jealousy for parents.

"What's wrong with me? I know Yvette's mother. I am ten times more understanding than she'll ever be."

Later when the kids finish with adolescence and feel truly separated enough, then they can come back and look to their parents for closeness (to a point) and guidance (to a point). But during adolescence they often do look elsewhere. And more often than not they are helped by these relationships.

Friends Are Everything

As teenagers turn away from home and parents they suddenly become much more vulnerable to the world beyond the home. This is where their future lies. They cared before about success and acceptance by friends, but now they care *intensely*. In order to feel good about themselves, in order to feel secure, they must see a place for themselves in that world, especially in relation to their friends. Their most intense highs and lows are now dictated by the success or failure of those friendships. Success in the classroom or in sports is very important, but true happiness for a teenager begins and ends with friends.

Fitting In—Girls

"Hi, Carla."

"Oh, hi, Janelle."

"Before you get too friendly, Carla, I just want you to know that the reason I called is that Shana, Annette, and I were talking and we decided that we don't want you to sit at our table at lunch anymore. We think that you're not popular enough, and that it will hurt us to have you sitting with us. So don't expect to eat lunch with us tomorrow."

"Lauren, Beth and I want to ask you something."

"Yeah?"

"Why is it that you sometimes wear sweaters that have stains on them?"

Valerie noticed at lunch that Robin and Debby seemed to be talking about her without including her. She had noticed more of this sort of thing lately, and she was worried. That night Valerie launched a counterattack.

"Oh, listen, Debby, I meant to tell you. The other day I was talking with Denise and she said that Robin had said to her that though you and she are real good friends and all, she thinks that sometimes you act real stuck-up. Robin made Denise promise not to tell, but you know how Denise blabs everything."

The whole story was, of course, a total lie. But Valerie hoped that maybe it would help drive a wedge between Robin and Debby.

Newly adolescent girls, forced by their adolescence to sep-

arate from their parents, are not confident. In time, they may
be. But the young teenage girl feels the ever-present threat that
she could lose it all. This underlying insecurity gives rise to
much cruelty. At the same time, teenage girls make strong,
almost loving attachments to girls that they admire, which
often creates intense jealousy. The result of this combination
of insecurity and strong attachments is an unparalleled nastiness. It is most clearly observed in the phenomenon of junior-
high cliques. (This is true with boys also, but not nearly to
the same extent.) Little can rival the viciousness and social
desperation of eleven- to fourteen-year-old girls.

The basic purpose of cliques is to give each group member
a sense of self-worth, which is inextricably tied to the exclu-
siveness of a clique. A clique can serve its purpose only
by being a clique, by excluding others, by putting them
down.

"We are better. Is there anybody else in our class who dresses
as good as us?"

The nastiness and the cliques existed prior to adolescence.
But with adolescence the need to find security and self-worth
outside the home increases dramatically. To an appalling degree their day-to-day feeling of self-worth is directly tied to a
sense of their own popularity. One wants to be accepted and
one also wants that acceptance to be as high on the social
ladder as possible.

"After Germaine Thurson, it is definitely either me or Beverly who is the second most popular girl in our class. I mean,
nobody can compete with Germaine."

And all of this transpires on a day-to-day, literally minute-
to-minute, basis. Where do I stand? Do they still like me? A
girl may take even the most casual remark from a friend in
class as a sign that something is wrong. And until explained,
the remark can become an obsession.

"Lisa, why did you say that my teeth looked funny today?"
"I don't know. I didn't mean anything by it."
"Are you sure?"
"Yeah."
"Oh. Okay. Want a breath mint?"

A not uncommon phenomenon is the teenage girl who simply does not have the toughness to endure the social meat grinder of the junior-high years and who, in effect, opts out. Such girls will often have mostly boys as friends, and will say quite openly that they simply find boys easier to get along with, more accepting, than girls.

Fortunately, this stage passes. By the middle of high school, girls have usually formed more lasting friendships and are content to be part of a small but secure group of friends. As they mature, the importance of being popular wanes, replaced by real, lifelong friendships. But that stage where popularity means everything can be a very nasty stage.

Fitting In—Boys

With boys it is a little different. Popularity and cliques are also part of their lives, but not to the same extent as with girls. Regarding friends, boys generally are easier. As long as a boy is not odd, in which case he runs the risk of being picked on, there are not too many requirements for acceptance. Before adolescence the two things that matter are being tough and being good at sports, with the latter probably being of primary importance. But what also matters is the ability to be fun to be with. Overall, adolescent boys very much enjoy their friends. Most teenage boys will usually say that "hanging around" with friends and partying are their favorite things to do.

However, with the onset of adolescence there does seem to come an upswing of competitive posturing. The years in junior high school seem to be the main time when boys have to fight a lot to show who is tougher. Or, more accurately, they have to talk a lot about fighting, with an occasional real fight thrown in.

"Tad Granger said that he's going to kick your ass."
"Yeah. Well, he's a fucking wimp. You tell him that I'm going to kick his ass."

And maybe they will fight, and maybe they won't. In a few years, the odds on fighting go way down. Fighting is admired less and less until, by high school, it's considered downright dumb to fight, unless the boys are drunk, in which case it is more acceptable, because it's part of being drunk, which is fine.

Cool replaces tough. Coolness—the capacity to be in style—is a kind of sexualized, downbeat version of tough. The need to be cool, to be in style, is probably the closest that boys come to teenage girls' obsession with looks. But this concern is different in that it is not nearly so demanding. One does not really have to be cool. Many boys do care about how they look and act, but mainly that caring has to do with trying to get girls, not with peer acceptance. For the most part, how a boy looks and dresses is not so much an issue of status as it is one of identification. How you look and dress indicates which general group you belong to: preppies, maggots, whatever.

In general, in regards to fitting in, teenage boys have it easier. They are easier for adults to get along with. Even with that apotheosis of teenage *un*coolness, the nerd (who is usually seen as a boy), social ostracism is just not that daunting. There are many nerdy teenage boys. That is, boys who just do not seem to care about being in style, or simply do not have a feel for it. And for the most part, they are not unhappy. They usually have a couple of friends, they do have interests that they enjoy, and in many ways they have an easier adolescence than their more self-conscious classmates. For social acceptance, boys are just not as demanding as girls.

The Tyranny of How I Look

Perhaps no other issue of adolescence can be quite so cruel as the tyranny exercised over adolescent girls by their own appearance.

"Mom, I'm not going to school today."

"What did you say, Tiffany?"

"I'm sick. I'm not going to school."

"You don't sound sick."

"Well, I am. And besides, I can't get my stupid hair to look right."

"It looks fine, Tiffany."

"No, it doesn't. Ever since I had it cut, it looks all wrong, and today I just can't make it look right at all."

"Well, I think it looks very nice. Now hurry up or you'll be late for school."

"I told you, Mom, I'm not going."

"Of course you are. You look fine."

"No, Mom. I'm not going to school."

Nor did she.

"Mom, I can't find my green sweater."

"It's at the cleaners, Theresa."

"What?"

"I said it's at the cleaners, dear."

"But it can't be."

"Well, it is."

"But then I have nothing to wear."

"You have your blue sweater."

"It has a spot on it."

"Well, what about that nice light blue one?"

"I can't wear that, Mom, it makes my breasts look too big. You know that. I have nothing to wear."

"You have lots of very nice clothes, Theresa, I'm sure you can find something."

"I can't."

"Mom, my face looks bumpy."

"No, it doesn't, dear."

"Yes, it does. I was just looking at it in the mirror and it definitely looks bumpy. Come here. Look at it in the mirror."

"I can't see anything, dear. Your face doesn't look bumpy to me."

"I don't know how you can't see it. It's bumpy."

Prior to adolescence girls care a lot about how they look, particularly as it relates to their feelings of acceptance by other girls their age. With adolescence the greater reliance on peers for their sense of self-worth combines with newly emergent sexual feelings to make "how I look" take on extraordinary importance.

Leaving the security of home, where there is no self-consciousness, and crossing over the threshold to go to school—where everyone sees you—can be overwhelming.

"Didn't Janice wear that green sweater yesterday? I didn't know her family was poor."

"Aren't Cheryl's cheeks fat? I never noticed it before. I don't know why not. She looks sort of like a chipmunk."

Girls at school do not *always* say or think these things, but every teenage girl going to school feels that they do. Certainly they know that they do it themselves.

Not only are teenage girls passionately self-conscious about how they look, but also most of them feel they are ugly, or at least less attractive than they really are. They feel this way for two main reasons. One, much of female sexuality is focused not on boys but on themselves, on how they feel about their own appearance. Male sexuality is just the opposite: it focuses most strongly on the object of desire. The second reason is cultural. In the United States girls are exposed from an early age to a world that says that it is a very good thing to be beautiful. Furthermore, television, movies, and magazines show exactly what beautiful is.

Girls know exactly what they are *supposed* to look like. And once they reach adolescence, the majority of girls become painfully aware that they fall far short of their ideal. The concern with their appearance for these girls can become a true burden. Many teenage girls get out of bed on school days an hour, even two hours earlier than necessary, just to work on getting themselves to look right.

"Now, Caroline, you really are an attractive girl."
"Sure, you would say that, you're my mother."

Nothing parents say seems to help. For teenagers, the only thing that matters is what their peers think. Caring intensely during early adolescence about how one looks is normal. And it can even be a source of pleasure. But it can also get out of hand. Anorexia is a psychological disorder wherein girls (and only rarely boys) starve themselves, sometimes fatally, in their conviction that they can never be thin enough. It is a disorder that occurs only once adolescence has begun. Prior to having sexual feelings, girls cannot be truly anorexic because the sexual feelings contribute so strongly to the obsession of never feeling quite thin enough.

The Typical Teenager

There is no fixed way of being a normal adolescent. A teenage boy may do household chores without being asked, a teenage girl may not argue at every turn, and such behavior would not necessarily suggest a need for immediate psychiatric hospitalization. But the gender-specific solutions to the dilemmas of adolescence described here are more than just the usual ways of coping with teenage years. They are dictated by very real psychological forces common to all adolescents. Much about adolescence differs from child to child, but much more is the same.

3

Being the Parent
of a Teenager

If establishing a sense of one's own independence is the main job of the adolescent, then letting go of their children is the main task of the parents of adolescents. It is not long before teenagers will be out on their own, and once out there they must be able to survive. Gradually, whether teenage children seem ready or not, they must be allowed to take over the controls of their own lives.

But the deepest impulse of their parents screams out against this duty.

"They are too young. They don't know what they are doing. The world is different today. It's so much more complicated, tougher, more dangerous."

Still, parents must let go, and, to make matters even trickier, they must do so while still setting limits and making demands. And often hardest of all for the parents of the basic belligerent teenager, love must still be given.

What is it to be the parent of a teenager? It is to do what

you think best—when really you have no idea what is best. It is to ride out the storms and be back again the next day. It is to give love to a child who does not seem to want it, to a child who five minutes ago seemed to deserve a punch more than anything else.

Letting Go

The capacity to let go, to separate, to allow a child to resolve his or her own destiny is crucial to being the parent of a teenager. But it is also hard. Parents of teenagers must somehow accept that a lot may go on *over which they have no control*. Their teenage children may drink, smoke, have sex, use drugs, and there may be little that the parents can do about it. Even less can they control the more generally uncooperative, obstreperous behavior which is the hallmark of adolescence.

It is during their teenage years that our offspring finally begin to resemble the adults they will become. Often enough, the initial indicators of the future are not at all what their parents had envisioned. We might like to change what we see, but cannot. It's too late. They're already launched. Nevertheless, parents must accept their adolescents for whom they have in fact become, rather than "punish" them for having become someone else entirely. Parents of teenagers must tolerate losing a child and, when the last child is gone from the household, being suddenly alone in a new way. The role of active parent that has defined their lives for the past eighteen or so years is stripped from them. Letting go is rarely easy.

Preventing Disaster

Prior to adolescence, when a child screws up the worst that can happen is that he will suffer. It's easy enough to pick up the pieces and go on to the next event. But during adolescence mistakes are not so easily forgotten or forgiven by the world. They can count. To do badly in school, to succumb to drugs or alcohol, to allow oneself to become pregnant, all can lead to problems affecting the rest of one's life. Mistakes in adolescence not only can hurt; they can cause problems that do not go away. Parents understand this, of course, and therefore letting go during this crucial period takes on a whole new meaning. This is the cruel irony: we are asked to let go precisely when the stakes go up.

Being the parents of adolescents is hard because children may have reached this stage without attaining the ability to work through problems well at all. It is one thing to let them fail so that they may ultimately learn how to succeed. It is another thing altogether to let them fail when there is no lesson to be learned, when the only outcome is . . . failure.

When my son Nick became a teenager I was especially aware of the above problems and I figured out a solution. Other parents have no doubt thought of it as well: if his mother and I restricted Nick to his room and checked on him regularly until it was time to go away to college, we could avoid all the problems. Unfortunately, Nick would not agree to this plan, and I also think there may be laws against it. (Could I have gotten away with four years of notes to teachers saying that Nick still had his cold, but assuredly would be in tomorrow?)

I have heard parents talk only half-jokingly of moving to a small town in North Dakota just to get away from all the bad things that could tempt or harm their children. (Of course, small towns in North Dakota have all of the above problems.)

But once a child becomes a teenager, he faces risks which simply did not exist before. These risks are heightened by the increased freedom and responsibility that one has to give teenagers, just because they *are* older, even if they do not seem ready for it.

The dangers that do exist are real. We can hope to guide our children, to protect them. But as teenagers, they are out in the real world—a world that has real dangers. This we have to accept. We cannot hold them back.

"Oh, yeah. Watch me. I just enrolled Jimmy in Miss Millicent's Academy. It's a boarding school fifteen miles from the nearest town and that town only has a laundromat. Also the biggest classes have four kids."

Letting Them Fail

Jeremy had a history report due on Monday. He kept putting off the job; only on Sunday night did he start. By then there simply was not enough time left.

On Monday morning Jeremy said he was sick and could not go to school.

"You didn't finish the history report, did you?"

"No. But that's not why. I really am sick."

"I don't believe you, Jeremy. You've done this before."

"But, Mom, if I go to school and don't hand in the assignment on time, it will drop me a full grade for the quarter. And you know I have to keep my grades up for college. Mom. Please. I swear to God, I won't ask for this again."

If Jeremy goes to school and does not hand in the assignment, his grade *will* go down. This could affect his final grade and make his high school transcript just that much less attractive to a college. It could make a difference. But should his parents keep bailing out Jeremy? If they do so, how would he ever learn responsibility? Unless they let him suffer the consequences of his laziness, how will he ever want to change?

This argument makes sense, but the reality is that Jeremy may not learn from his mistakes in any event. He may simply continue to delay assignments, be forced to go to school anyway, and get substantially lower grades as a result. He may indeed jeopardize his chances of admission to college.

So, should Jeremy's parents let him stay home to finish the history project?

Janine's father noticed that she was often very bossy when she was with her best friend, Darcy. He commented on this to Janine. But the bossiness continued. And in fact Darcy eventually broke off the friendship.

Janine then found a new "best" friend, but she was also bossy with this new girl. Janine's father observed this behavior and was tempted to intervene. After all, his daughter was sowing the seeds for another failed relationship. But should he intervene?

Unfortunately there comes a time when it is no longer appropriate for parents to rescue their children. Sometimes children are going to fail and parents simply have to let it happen, not because this is the only way teenagers will ever learn anything, but simply because it's time for them to proceed with their own destinies whether *or not* they learn anything in the process.

The problem of separation is not, of course, isolated in adolescence. Within all of us there remains a vestige of the baby self that does not like to separate, that does not like to be independent. For parents, children provide a new source of attachment. And though our children get older and inevitably grow away from us, the process of *our* growing away from *them* is not as certain. We get used to their loving us and needing us. They can even become the central meaning in our lives. This can be a dangerous passion, because they *will* leave home. Then what? We may find that we have very little left. Fearing this, knowing this, we can become unwilling to give them up. We can become inappropriately involved in their needs. We can feel that our continuing supervision is necessary to them, while in fact it's necessary only to us.

"You're wrong. My Gretchen cannot manage without me. If I weren't always watching over her, God knows what would happen to her. She certainly can't run her own life. Ask anybody."

Maybe Gretchen can't run her own life, but at some point her mother has to let go and let her daughter make a muddle of things. She can hope to guide Gretchen, to protect her, but she absolutely must not hold her back. She must let go.

"But I'm not going to stand and watch while she screws up her whole life."

After a certain point, that is exactly what parents have to do.

Accepting Them for Themselves

We love our children and we enjoy them. At the same time, we have expectations for them. We take pleasure in their successes and are disappointed by their failures—not just for them but for ourselves. Our egos ride on how well our kids do.

"But that's terrible. Parents should be happy for who their children are, not for how successful they are."

True, but feelings of pride and indirect glory are normal. The problems come not from these feelings, but from *what we do* with these feelings.

Molly was getting C's and D's in high school. Her parents wanted her to go to college but Molly was ambivalent. She preferred to hang around with her friends or, when home, to watch television or talk on the telephone.

One day Molly and her mother were carrying a heavy table up from the basement. When Molly stumbled, an edge of the table scraped against the wall, digging into the plaster.

"Watch it, Molly. Can't you do anything right?"

"I tripped. It was an accident."

"You don't watch where you're going. You're not careful about anything. You don't care about anything."

"Mom, I'm sorry, it was an accident."

"You can pay for it. I work hard. What do you do? All you do is talk on the phone and hang out with your loser friends. You're not going to do anything with your life. You don't care about anything. And do you know what? I don't really care what happens to you."

"Fuck you, Mom. You're right, I don't care about anything. I don't care about helping you with your table."

And Molly left her mother with the table halfway up the cellar stairs.

"Come back here. Don't you dare talk to me that way."

As Molly's mother tried to figure out what to do about the table, she also wondered why she had become so angry.

As parents, we have a sense that our children are in a changing state, like wet and still moldable clay. They are still forming, not yet finished. Their flaws as young children are easier to accept because these flaws may change.

Yet by the time of adolescence there are areas in which the

clay has already hardened, where our children have become the final product, the adult they will be forever. A problem for parents of adolescents is that they begin to realize that their children are not so much *on their way* to becoming something. In some respects they have already arrived at their destination—the permanent adult form.

A sixth-grade girl who is lazy about homework and gets C's is a child who is a lazy C student. But a high-school junior who is lazy about homework and gets C's and D's is someone for whom many avenues are now cut off. She could still go to college or become rich or famous, but her chances have started to narrow. A teenager who does not care about school and just wants to have a good time is not what her parents wanted.

"No, that's not true. I just want her to be happy."

Many parents genuinely feel this way, but most, deep down, also feel disappointment when their teenagers accomplish little and, further, do not seem to care. We want them to be successful, to be great. Often we want for them the success that we had wanted for ourselves. We may transfer our own frustrated goals onto our children. This too is normal. And it is not bad.

Often our children do not live up to our hopes for them. They rarely can, and often we are disappointed. This too is also normal and not bad. But sometimes we take our disappointment out on our children. This may be normal but it is *not* okay. It's not fair to our children to get angry at them because they have not become what we had wanted. That's our problem, not theirs.

To deal with this problem we must first recognize it. We must openly admit our disappointment in what they have become. This admission is the most important step, and one that we are often reluctant to take. It carries a certain depressing finality: "This is it, this ends my hope. I wasn't the big success I wanted to be and now Molly's not going to be either."

We must allow ourselves to feel bad and grieve for what might have been: "She's not going to be anybody special. She's just going to be Molly."

Only after we have admitted to ourselves our disappointment and allowed ourselves to feel bad about it can we refrain from taking out our feelings on our children. And *that* is the only fair thing to do.

Dealing with the Day-to-Day

Setting Limits

"Let me try to explain to you. It's not that I hate my parents. It's not that I think they are bad parents. I know they love me, and that what they do they really think is in my best interest. It's just that I feel trapped.

"I know that I'm young and that my judgment is not perfect and that I'm going to make mistakes. But they make mistakes too. And I'm not a little kid anymore. I have a brain and I've been through a lot. There was a lot of stuff that I went through, and they weren't involved at all, and it came out all right.

"The problem is that I can't stand them telling me what to do. I can't stand that there are rules, even if I break them.

"You don't know what it's like. When I'm alone in the house, I'm happy. I don't do anything wrong, at least nothing real bad. But as soon as they walk in the house I hate the place. It's like suddenly there's a weight pressing on me. I'd run away, but where would I go? I would love, really love, to have an apartment of my own. I could manage. They'd be surprised.

And then maybe I would go to school and maybe I wouldn't, but it would be my decision.

"You can't know how much I want to be on my own. I would be so happy."

To be left alone—this is the teenager's dream. Yet is it a delusion? In general, the judgment of a teenager is not as good as that of an adult. Adolescents simply have not been through it before. Even with parental controls teenagers will still make bad decisions, but without such controls there is no question they would make even more bad decisions.

However, heading off bad decisions is not the only issue in setting limits. Teenagers truly believe that they absolutely do not want controls, and that without them they would do just fine, but the fact is that controls do act as a source of *unacknowledged* security for them. Total responsibility for one's life is a burden. With total freedom one has to bear the full brunt of worrying about making the right decisions. There is something nice and secure (though, at another level, also infuriating) in the knowledge that there are one or two adults around who are *also* making decisions about what is best for you. Without this guidance the full burden of responsibility could cause more stress than most teenagers can or wish to handle. It's hard enough being a teenager without having to take on the *entire* responsibility for your own welfare.

"That's what you say, jerk. But I don't need my parents. And if you would all get the hell off my back, I would do just fine."

Teenagers fervently wish that their parents would leave them alone. They hate their parents' rules and constantly rail against them. They hate their parents' concern.

"I'll do fine. I don't need them to look after me."

And yet it is precisely this parental concern which assures that their children do not feel alone. This concern is what we can give them in their adolescence. So long as parents continue to be concerned, to try to look out for their teenager's welfare, the teenager can still at least somewhat feel like a child.

"So long as you are going to boss me around, you are going to protect me": they will not think this, but they will understand it, deep inside. This knowledge allows them to keep at least somewhat alive the fantasy that they are invulnerable, safe, under their parents' wing.

And we do want this for them. We do not want to force our children to grow up too soon, and before they are ready. We want our teenagers to take on increasing responsibility for their own lives, but not all the responsibility. They are still too young. It is more than they can handle. We do not want them to carry the full weight of the world on their shoulders. Not yet.

Parents of teenagers have an odd role. They fight to control their teenagers, but with inadequate weapons. And after a few years of heated but at best only partially successful battling, they give the control over to their children anyway. They are then young adults. So what's the point of those few years of struggle?

The point is those few years—a crucial few years in which, we hope, our children will mature. Regardless, they will be out on their own all too soon.

Making Decisions

Vanessa was supposed to get a lift home from the party at Karyn's and be back home by 11:30. At 11:20 Vanessa called.

"Hi. I'm just leaving the party. Can I sleep over at Leslie's house?"

Vanessa's parents know Leslie. They have nothing against Vanessa's staying at her house. On the other hand, this request is sudden. Why couldn't she have set up the plan before? Is there something else going on? For example, is Vanessa really trying to stay at the party until much later? What is the right thing for Vanessa's parents to say?

"Let me know quick," Vanessa adds. *"Somebody else wants to use the phone."*

At the last minute Vance gets tickets to the Alarm concert, one of his favorite groups. It was a school night and his parents knew that the next day he had a history test. Should Vance's parents allow him to go?

What is the correct time to expect a fourteen-year-old to come home from a Friday-night party? 9:30? 10:00? 10:30? None of the above?

A problem with raising teenagers is that you are constantly put in the position of having to make on-the-spot decisions, without having the vaguest idea as to the correct thing to do. Further, any decision that goes against the teenager holds the threat of an immediate, unpleasant, and protracted scene.

An important key with teenagers is understanding that it is often impossible to know what the best course of action is, or even whether there is a "best course." Yet a parent nonetheless has to make decisions, and quickly.

"Yes, you can stay overnight at Leslie's."

or

"No, you have to come home right now."

And if the latter decision, a protest will probably follow.

"No, Dad. I'm just going to be at Leslie's. You're being unreasonable."

Parents cannot always know what is best. No one can. They will make mistakes. But who better than they should be making decisions about their own child's life? They are the experts on their child and they, more than anyone, have their child's interest most at heart. Ultimately, parents must base a decision on what they feel comfortable with, and then stay with it. They alone have the task of making decisions regarding their children. That's the job. Parents cannot always be right; they can only do their best. Most important of all, in most situations it does *not* matter what decision parents make. The key is to do what they think is right, and adopt a firm, positive posture.

The problems arise when parents waver or get defensive. Then the teenager, recognizing uncertainty, moves in for the kill.

"I don't know, Wesley, you decide. What do you think is an appropriate curfew for you on Friday nights?"

"Four a.m., except if it turns out that there's a really good party. Then I don't have to come back until the next day."

Being a strong parent does not mean that one cannot reverse a decision. Parents *can* change their minds. The trick is in making certain that this about-face is seen as an autonomous, thoughtful decision, not as a result of being bullied. There can be a fine but significant line between the two. It is okay to be swung by a child's arguments. But the change should come because of the *content* of the argument, not because of the desire to avoid a hassle.

"Oh, Dad, I'm not going to do anything at Leslie's. You just don't like me to change plans. That's no reason. Please can't I stay at Leslie's?"

Maybe Vanessa's father does decide that Vanessa is right. He doesn't like a fast change of plans. And maybe he is not worried about her staying over at Leslie's. If so, he loses nothing by changing his mind.

The problem comes with children who know that they can bully their parents. Given the opportunity, they will do just that, time after time.

"Don't ignore me, Dad. It's not fair and you know it. You always let Kevin stay out later."

"Vanessa, we've gone through all this before. I don't want to talk about it."

"You don't want to talk about it because you know you're wrong. And I'm not going to stop talking about it until you change your mind, because it really is unfair. I can't believe you're doing this to me. I can't."

"Vanessa, please try to be reasonable."

"Reasonable? You're the one who's not being reasonable. You are just being so unfair."

"Now, Vanessa."

"Yes, you are. You are so unfair. I can't stand it."

"Oh, all right, Vanessa. Have it your way. But there just better not be any funny business about this."

"Thanks, Dad. I love you a lot. I'll call you in the morning when I need to be picked up. Bye."

Children of parents who cannot be bullied will also argue, and they too will push—but not nearly so hard, because they have learned that it won't work with their parents.

How does a child know whether a change resulted from her bullying or from a parent's independent decision? In any given instance, she may not. But over time, over repeated instances, children learn whether theirs are parents who make decisions based on what they think is best or on what they think their children will accept without a tantrum.

The key in decision making is that parents make decisions and that these decisions be their own, right or wrong.

"But sometimes I just don't have the time or the will. I know I shouldn't, but I give in to her rather than get into a huge fight. I let her win because I just don't have the energy."

This is the truth. The rule about not letting oneself be bullied is not an absolute rule. On occasion, with very persistent teenagers, parents just do not feel like "getting into it" day after day. If the issue is not crucial, you can concede in order to avoid yet another onslaught of teenage abuse. In fact, if you're not up to a battle it is often better to avoid that route altogether, rather than entering the argument only to get worn down.

However, parents must not *always* avoid the fights. To do so is to abrogate the role of parent. Parents are free to pick the times and issues on which they will make a stand. In fact, there must be times when they do just that. And when they do fights will inevitably follow.

Gentle Nudges

But a parent's role is not always to keep the teenager under control; sometimes it is to give him a little push.

Jeffrey had been talking about trying out for the basketball team, but clearly he had mixed feelings. He very much liked basketball, but he was a marginal candidate for the team. He dreaded the humiliating possibility of being cut from the team. The sign-ups were scheduled for Saturday at 1 a.m. At 10 a.m. he announced he was not going.

"I don't have the right form to fill out. You can only get the forms during the week. I can't go."

"Yes, you can, Jeffrey. I'm sure that they can work something out."

"No, they won't let me. They said kids had to bring the form. I can't go."

"Jeffrey, if you want to try out for the team, I'm sure it will work out."

"No, I'm not going."

Jeffrey's parents, however, did not back off, and they finally convinced him, over his objections, to go to the sign-ups.

"Jeffrey, you have nothing to lose. The worst that can happen is that you can't sign up."

They did work something out. Jeffrey made the team, barely, and he was happy about it.

One reason for children's success is that they have parents who have cared all along the way about their succeeding and have constantly communicated this caring. Jeffrey's parents knew how much he loved basketball, felt pretty sure he could make the team, but also knew he needed a gentle nudge to get past his lack of confidence about trying out.

Other parents do more than just nudge. These are the proverbial tennis mothers, football fathers, parents who forever prod, who tell their children, explicitly or otherwise, "I want you to do well in school and move yourself up the way I was never able to do."

These are not bad parents. Successful adults often genuinely thank such parents, recognizing that had they not been pushed, they would not have been so successful.

But the prodding can be a two-edged sword. While pushing

often yields positive results, there are risks. Sometimes, children who have experienced success choose to stop achieving.

"I don't understand. Right in his senior year he quit hockey and just hung around with his jerky friends. He could have been all-league. How could he do this to me?"

If we hang our hopes on our children, we must be aware that it is a burden for them.

"I don't really care so much about how I do, but I don't want to disappoint Dad."

In the end everything may work out, with everyone happy. But if what we want is not just for them but for ourselves as well, we must recognize this. We may not sacrifice our children to our unfulfilled dreams.

Giving Too Much

It is appropriate to make sacrifices of one's time and energy for one's children, but only to a point.

Giving is fine, necessary, but parents who run themselves ragged doing things for their children may be setting themselves up for disappointment. A problem with giving too much of oneself to a teenager is that if she does not pay you back— and often adolescents do not—a parent can feel very hurt. And this can make for trouble, because when parents get too hurt, they can also get too mad.

"I just don't care about Denise anymore. I look at her and I feel nothing. After what I did for her, this is how she pays me back. She has hurt me too much."

This attitude is unjustified, a sign of a parent who let matters get out of hand.

Parents are allowed not to do something for their teenage children simply because they don't feel like it. There may be times when a teenager has been so lazy and/or obnoxious that his parent is just too angry to do any favors.

"Take you to the mall? I wouldn't even sit in the same car with you, Dennis. Just get away from me. I can't stand the sight of you."

Teenagers will survive such refusals. It also reminds them that you're human and that humans can get quite angry if pushed by very obnoxious teenagers. This is a perfectly useful lesson for teenagers.

Adolescence is a time of increasing separation between parent and child. The parents who do too much for their child may ultimately get in the way of that process. Too many gifts come with too many strings that bind parent to child. Parents need to know when to say, "No."

Calming the Waves of Hysteria

But again, perhaps the hardest part about being the parent of a teenager is that though parents must let go, they must also be there to provide love and support.

Fourteen-year-old Jennifer had been invited to a party at her friend Sharon's house on Friday night. However, her parents had already made family plans with her grandparents.

"But I can't miss the party. I have to go."
"Nobody has to go to a party, Jennifer. There will be other parties. We haven't had supper at your grandparents' in a long time."
"But you don't understand. All of the kids are going to be there. I can't miss the party. I just can't."

"I am sorry, Jennifer. But I am not going to discuss it further. You will go with us Friday night."

"No, Dad. I can't. Dad! Dad! I can't! I have to go to Sharon's party!"

"No, Jennifer. You're coming with us."

"DAD!"

"For God's sake, Jennifer. It's just a party."

Not to Jennifer. It is far more than that.

Teenagers have a lot of trouble seeing past now. Because they have only just started what they consider their adult life, they simply do not have the experience that comes with living. Thus they lack one crucial piece of wisdom: nothing makes such a big difference. They do not yet know that somehow things almost always have a way of working out—though how that may be may seem incomprehensible at the time. The tomorrows keep coming, never so dramatically different from the yesterdays. But teenagers can get murderously hung up on the dilemmas of now. It is a real and a serious problem.

Jennifer in regard to her party:

"All of my friends are going to be there. If I don't go, then everybody will have been there except me. It's like I won't be part of what's going on. And then in school, they'll talk about the party, except I won't have been there. I'll be out of it. And then maybe because I wasn't there, they'll think I'm a baby or something, and maybe they won't be friendly with me the way they were before. I mean, they'll still be friendly, but I won't be in with them like I am now. You see, I have to go, or lose everything."

Teenagers' lack of perspective can be scary. Here parents have an important role. Since they do have a better sense of reality than their children, they need to keep stating what that reality is. It can make a difference.

"You will not lose your friends because you don't go to one party."

"I will! I will! You don't understand."

"No, Jennifer, you will not lose your friends. They will still like you, even if you miss the party."

And maybe Jennifer will hear some of this. And maybe she will be reassured.

The Unconditional Deal

The behavior of some teenagers can be so horrible and so disruptive they may need to be moved out of the home. I'll discuss these kids later. Most adolescents are just normal horrible and they still deserve our unconditional love.

I will yell at my kids when they are obnoxious to me because I do not like it, and I do not want them to act that way, and I want to let them know that being obnoxious to me is unacceptable. But another part of me says that it is okay. Although I may hate their obnoxiousness I will defend their right to be that way. They are still children, *my* children. And I will love them regardless, unconditionally.

I Never Used to Act That Way

"Vera, would you please come into the kitchen and help me put away these dishes?"

"Why?"

A voice in Vera's mother's head hears this exchange and comments: "I never used to act that way. When Mom would ask me to do something like that, I always did it. I didn't like doing it, but I always did it. I don't understand. I just don't seem to be able to control Vera and Reggie in the way that Mom could control us."

And of course, her mother, who now lives five blocks away, comments on this too: "I don't know what your problem is, Edith, the way you let Vera and Reggie talk to you. We never let you and Richard talk that way."

"But I don't let them talk that way, Mom."

"Well, you must be doing something wrong."

Parents of teenagers today have an ongoing sense that "I am not really in control of what's going on. I deal with it, but I am really not sure that I am doing anything right."

With most teenagers, nothing does go terribly wrong, so the day-to-day sense of inadequacy is tempered by the thought: "Whatever I might be doing wrong can't be too serious." But even with those parents whose teenagers seem to be functioning just fine, there often remains an ongoing lack of true confidence about one's skills. These parents are doing quite well; they just do not realize it. Why?

For one thing, today's teenagers do face "new" challenges that parents sense are constantly lurking. Drugs are a relatively new problem. Teenagers do have sex earlier (but some parents were members of the first generation for which the rules about sex began to change).

But the main reason for parental uncertainty is their memory of their own childhood. When most parents think back they remember, correctly in many cases, that they did not behave toward their parents in the way that their children behave toward them. They *were* obedient. They did not talk nearly so boldly as their own children. From this comparison parents often conclude that the difference is their own failure as a parent. To make matters worse, the living presence of one's own parents may also emphasize the point.

"Maybe you just don't have a feel for it, Elaine. I know you, Clarence, and Emily would never have behaved like your kids."

But parents' comparisons with their own adolescence are usually not valid. As discussed, today's teenagers do have more of a general sense of entitlement—an entitlement that includes talking back—but they feel this way because their parents have chosen to let them.

So comparisons with adolescence past may determine that parents of today are doing a lousy job, but the comparisons ignore the fact that it's a different ball game today, and parents themselves changed the rules.

It *is* harder, it *does* require more effort for the parents of today to get the same nice behavior from their children as their parents elicited. But the question of how today's adolescents will turn out as adults is a separate matter. It is crucial for parents to continue to demand of their children what they believe is appropriate. Their immediate results—their teenagers' behavior—may not match their own at the same age, but in the long run, so long as they continue to make the appropriate demands, their children should turn out just as well. Who knows, maybe even better.

II

Between Parent and Teenager

For those who have never raised a teenage child, it is hard to imagine the day-to-day swings between crazed frenzy and genuine tranquillity. Some of the time things are calm, even beautiful. You love your kid and he or she seems just fine. But at other times, perhaps five minutes later, you behave like a crazed person, enraged beyond reason, and at the same time certain your child is utterly doomed, so warped in character development as to stand no chance of making it in life. And then things are fine again.

Crises can arise with dazzling suddenness, seemingly out of nothing. Parents can feel very much on the spot, needing an immediate strong and correct response, but having no idea what that response should be. Teenagers feel that they would be fine if parents left them alone forever, but parents feel that curfews must be set, dirty clothes must be picked up, and siblings restrained from beating each other into unconsciousness.

"*How would Bill Cosby have dealt with this?*"

"*I wonder how Queen Elizabeth acted when her kids behaved this way.*"

It is often difficult to know the correct thing to do, and often even more difficult to do it, especially when you feel enraged, betrayed, belittled, and depressed. And then the next day comes and Emily seems fine and you can't remember exactly what the problem was.

4

◆

Communication and Trust

Surely, communication and trust are the foundation of any parent-teenager relationship, or maybe not. The adolescent mandate demands that teenagers separate from their parents. Adolescents, especially boys, want to say little to and hear less from their parents. And in order to keep their parents out of their lives, teenagers can be very sneaky about what they are doing. Yet parents are often told that communicating with their teenager children is vital. It is a subject rife with misunderstanding.

Communication

"Well, son, what's happening?"
"Not too much, Dad. The usual."
"How's school going?"
"Pretty good, but I'm still having a tough time with algebra. I just don't know if I can ever get the hang of it."

"You know, I felt that way about algebra when I was in high school. I remember really getting down about it. But I hung in there, and finally it ended up okay."

"Thanks, Dad, I really like hearing about what it was like when you were in school. Maybe I'll do okay in algebra too."

The above conversation has never happened. Never. In the whole history of the world. Parents do communicate with teenagers, but usually more along the lines of "Don't forget to take the microwave dinners out of the freezer before you go to school, Janis."

Or: "Eleven-thirty means eleven-thirty and I want you in then!"

Or: "Mom, can I have five bucks?"

Or perhaps: "Get out of my room!"

The fact that communication between parent and teenager lacks both quantity and quality is not necessarily a sign that anything is wrong. Nor is the fact that conversations are often one-sided, with only parents doing the talking, a danger signal.

Listening to Your Teenager—I

There is a profound difference between listening to one's children while setting limits and making demands and listening at all other times.

With younger children the rule about listening is fairly straightforward.

"Rodney, Lucinda has a school project to do tonight and I want you to do the dishes for her out of turn."

"That's not fair. You never had her do it when I had a school project."

"I want you to do it tonight."

"But it's not fair. You never make exceptions for me. Only

*for her. Why does she always have to be the one who gets the
special treatment and never me? She gets out of everything and
I never get out of anything. You really favor her. It's not fair.
I never get anything for me. Only her. Why is it? Answer me!"*

With younger children the rule is simple: in limit-setting
situations, do not listen. To ask "Do you really feel that way,
Rodney, that we favor Susan?" is to invite disaster. The message Rodney hears is "Please go on fussing, but with greater
passion and length, and maybe I will get so mad that I will
send you to your room instead of making you do the dishes."

In limit-setting situations younger children will say anything, resort to anything, either to avoid doing what is asked
of them or to break down a rule: "I hate you. I'm the only kid
in my whole school who can't stay up to watch *Pistol Cops*.
The other kids think I'm weird. I'm not going to go to school
anymore. I'm not."

The parent simply cannot listen to these remarks. If your
child is bringing up real issues they will also arise at another
time, or you can ask. Parents make decisions relating to
younger children totally on their own. *Consulting* with children courts disaster.

With adolescents, however, the situation is trickier. Since
they are now semi-adults they must be accorded a new status.
What they say—even when the words may be manipulative
nonsense—must be given some respect, some validity. It does
not do to completely ignore a teenager. But, you say, your
teenager doesn't respect you. It doesn't matter. You are the
adult. He is the child. Respect is learned where it is given.

*"But, Mom, I know I just got the new boots, but . . . Now
don't get mad, listen to me. I can't wear the same new boots
when I go out on weekends because it will look stupid. All the
kids will know that those are the same new boots I wore during*

the week in school. They'll think we're poor. It will be very embarrassing to me. This other pair of boots I saw are a little more expensive, but they really are a good value."

Sometimes what they say is nonsense, designed to infuriate, but sometimes it is not.

"I know it means staying out way past my curfew. But the band doesn't even start playing until eleven, and they're the group I want to hear. I will be with Melissa, Danielle, and Kenny the whole time, and Danielle's father has agreed to pick us up right at one-fifteen when it's over. It's totally safe. I know that's very late. But I don't have school the next day or anything."

Sally's parents should not necessarily say yes, but certainly they should listen. Sally's argument is a good one.

What should parents do when they have taken a stand and their teenager starts to argue against it? A good rule is to listen up to a point. Listen to their initial argument. See if it makes sense. If it does, genuinely consider it. Parents lose nothing by changing their mind. But if the argument does not seem reasonable, or if the parent, after due consideration, decides to stay with the original decision anyway, then discussion must cease. Listening must end.

"Carolyn, I'm sorry, but you can't get the second pair of boots."
"But the ones I have aren't nice enough for weekends."
"No, Carolyn, you can't get them."
"But you don't understand. The ones I have really . . ."

The parent should say no more. If Carolyn continues to badger, just leave. Once a decision truly has been made, separation should be a parent's only goal.

"You're not listening to me!"
"That's right."

Listening to Your Teenager—II

When not setting limits, parents should always be available to listen. Sometimes teenagers really do want to communicate with their parents. They want to tell them of concerns, fears, things their parents do that truly bother them.

It does no harm even to offer: "If there *ever* is something that you want to talk to me about, I will listen." Many adolescents may never take their parents up on these offers. But letting your teenage children know that you are available to listen can be an invaluable support to them.

And listening means listening, not giving advice. But if parents say this, they must mean it.

"They Don't Listen to Anything I Say"

"Eloise, I think it would be a good idea if you dropped Spanish. You're spending a lot of time on it, and you're still failing. I'm afraid it's pulling your other grades down as well."

"No, Dad, I can handle it. Just leave me alone. You don't know anything. I'm doing okay."

"No, Eloise, you're starting to do badly, and I think the Spanish is just too much."

"Dad! I can handle it. I'm doing okay. Now leave me alone."
Two nights later:

"Dad, I've decided to drop Spanish. I was talking to Becky's mother about how I was having trouble in school and she said maybe I should drop Spanish. I think she's right. Besides, I don't need it anyway, and now I'll have more time for my other subjects."

"What did I just say to you two nights ago?"
"I don't remember."

This is one aspect of being a parent that is particularly frustrating. As adults we feel that we are wiser than our teenage children. We have gone through it all before, and we know what is going to happen. In truth, we really can foresee some things to which our children are totally blind. Little stuff: "If you like this blouse, get it. Don't go looking into all the other stores. You know how you are. You'll only become more uncertain, and you'll end up not buying anything." And big things: "You say you can judge whether you've had too much to drink and shouldn't drive, but you can't."

Teenagers do not seem able to hear us even when we are right and when our words are in their best interest. They might listen to someone else, as in Eloise's case, but they also make wrong decisions and suffer from those decisions. From a parent's point of view, all the hassle could have been avoided had they only been able to listen. Furthermore, even if it turns out that we were absolutely right about what would happen and they were totally wrong—"Okay, you were right about *that*. But you still don't really understand, Dad"—this was to them an exception, proving nothing.

To take our advice, they feel, compromises their independence. To take parental advice and, worse yet, to recognize its helpfulness feels to a teenager like defeat. It is a defeat of all that they are trying to do, to establish that they can make decisions on their own. To have made a right decision because of parental advice is often for a teenager less desirable than to have failed on one's own.

"What good is it to me if it's not something I figured out on my own?"

"The last thing that I want is for my parents to be right, for them to be helpful. I don't want to need them."

What can we do? We should keep trying. Parents should give advice. If they see possible trouble, they should warn against it. Although teenagers cannot tolerate listening to advice or following it, they may heed it nonetheless. Sometimes good advice may slip through. Parents do have some influence over their teenagers, though not nearly as much as parents would like. As adolescence wanes and teenagers' independence is established, once again they will hear us. But not until then.

They Think I'm Always Criticizing (Them)

"Justin, will you be going out later?"

"I've done all the homework that I'm supposed to do. You don't always have to check up on me."

"What?"

"I'm not running out on stuff. I've done everything I'm supposed to."

"No, Justin, I wasn't thinking of anything like that. I just wondered if you were going past a store, could you pick me up some disposable razors."

"Sure you were, Dad."

"No, really, Justin."

"Why are you looking at me like that, Mom?"

"Like what, Sheila?"

"You know like what. You're giving me that look that says you're pissed off about something. I can tell what you're thinking."

"Honestly, Sheila, I wasn't thinking about you at all. If you must know, I was thinking about socks."

"Sure, Mom."

It is common that adolescents often assume critical thoughts on the part of their parents when their parents had no such thoughts at all. As a result, parents often find themselves in very frustrating conversations with their teenage children, who seem totally unable to hear what they are saying. It is as if their children are hearing some other voice.

"But, Rachel, I really don't mind if you go with Cheryl or not."
"You don't like her because she gets bad grades."
"I didn't even know she got bad grades."
"But now you do mind. Right?
"Rachel, don't put words into my mouth."

One consequence of teenagers' turning away from their parents is that they no longer really hear us. Instead they hear a little voice in their head that they think is ours but is not. It is their version of us. Actually, it is their new teenage *conscience*, only they do not know this yet. This conscience does not talk with their own voice, as it will by the end of adolescence, but with ours.

The voice they hear is often an inaccurate reflection of our thoughts. Their conscience was formed gradually over the course of childhood. Our voice was part of that formation, but much of a child's conscience develops independently of his parents, and by adolescence much of it may have little similarity to how we think.

Often the teenager's own conscience can be stricter and more demanding than the parents'. Some teenagers drive themselves far beyond our expectations, especially in school or in sports. Others reject the overly strict voice of their conscience, which they believe is ours but isn't.

"Fuck all of them. I'm sorry I can't be Mr. Perfect like they want. From now on I'm gonna do what I want, and if they don't like it, fuck 'em."

Part of adolescence is the development of one's own set of values. It is a sorting-out process, deciding what to accept from the parents' values and what to reject. The finished product at the end of adolescence is a set of values that are distinctly the teenager's own. But early on that process can be very confusing. Inevitably it can include stupid battles in which children fight about things parents never said and in which parents seem totally unable to correct this confusion.

Is Communication Impossible?

Contrary to the more general rule, sometimes parents and teenagers can and do talk, and such communication can be a positive experience for both.

"It was weird. Dad and I were driving down to Aunt May's to pick up a desk and we just started talking. About all kinds of stuff. I don't think I've ever talked with Dad like that in my life. I mean, I saw him as a regular person. I liked it, but it was weird."

The only problem is that it's hard to have such talks fit into any specific time frame. They happen when they happen. Planning to talk is a good idea, but parents must be ready to accept that such episodes do not usually work out as they wish.

"I'm sorry, Mom, I really do want to talk with you, and I do appreciate your wanting us to communicate, but I'm just not in the mood for it now. Maybe tomorrow, okay?"

"Please, son, I'll pay you ten dollars if you will just sit and listen to my story about the time in high school when I was so certain that I was going to get at least all B's that I actually made a bet with my father. I just know that this story will be valuable for you."

"Dad!"

Trusting Your Lying Teenager

"Trust is the foundation of the relationship between parent and teenager. Parents must be able to trust their children. Adolescents must feel trusted, for it is a key to their sense of self-respect."

This credo sounds reasonable but the words have little application to real life with teenagers. Trust is to adolescence what fairness is to childhood. Teenagers, truly believing in their cause, make trust the number one issue with which they hit their parents over the head. And on this issue parents really are vulnerable, because they also truly feel that trust is important:

"If we can't trust them as adolescents, when can they be trusted?"

"That's right. They have to trust me now. It really is important to me that they trust me. It's a way that they can show that they understand that I'm not a kid anymore, that I am older."

Those are valid points. The reality of adolescence, however, is that a lot of lying and sneaking around goes on. Teenagers lie regularly about the details of where they are going and what they are going to do. They also do many forbidden things which elude their parents' discovery. About those infractions there's nothing parents can do. The issue is what to do when you do find out.

Fifteen-year-old Justin received warning notices in English and geometry. He was supposed to bring them home, have his parents sign them, and then return the notices to school. Instead he threw them out. Two weeks later the school called to ask why the warning notices had not been returned.

"Justin, I got a call today and you're failing English and geometry. You never brought the warning notices home."

"They never gave them to me."

"Justin, you're lying."

"They never did. They're supposed to give them to me, but they never gave them to me. They must have forgot. I don't know. I never got them."

"Of course they did. That's ridiculous. The school said they were given to you."

"I didn't get them, Dad."

On Friday evening sixteen-year-old Lisa said she was going to Beverly's house for the night. "It's just going to be me and Beverly and I think Kristen. I'll call you in the morning if I need a ride home."

By chance Lisa's mother called Lisa at Beverly's house to remind her of a haircut appointment the next morning.

"No, Lisa and Beverly aren't here. Lisa said you knew that they were going to a party at Carrie's."

Confronted by her furious parents the next day, Lisa explained:

"It came up at the last moment. Yes, I did call you, twice, but the line was busy. Then I didn't know what to do, so I thought it would be okay. I didn't know that Carrie's parents weren't going to be home. But I wasn't going to leave once I

*got there. Besides, I wasn't doing anything wrong. I wasn't
drinking. Only Beverly was."*

*"I can't believe you can stand there and lie right to our faces.
We weren't on the phone."*

"Well, the line was busy. I did call."

*"You planned it the whole time. You knew we wouldn't let
you go, and you lied to Mrs. Pendleton as well."*

"I did not. She must have misunderstood."

*"You're incredible. You just lie and keep lying. How can you
do this? Do you think we're idiots? How can you just stand
there and lie like that?"*

"You don't believe anything I say. You don't trust me."

"Don't trust you? Don't trust you?"

"I'm not lying!"

"I don't know what to do with you."

"I hate you."

The problem is that teenagers (in fact, all children) lie a
lot, especially when they have been discovered doing what
they were not supposed to do. Sometimes they continue to lie
even when the facts are undeniable.

*"He still said he never saw the warning notices, even after
we found them crumpled up in his wastepaper basket."*

Just as long as they think they have even a *remote* chance
of being believed, they will lie. They will become outraged
when disbelieved when telling the truth, and just as outraged
when they are lying. It is a paradox. They know they are lying,
of course, but are still furious at their parents for not believing
them.

*"You don't trust me. I don't believe you don't trust me. I'm
going to be seventeen in June. I cannot believe that you are
saying this to me."*

"It's not the point that I'm lying. I'm old enough now that they should respect me enough to trust me. That I was lying has nothing to do with it."

If the trustworthiness of teenagers is the foundation of integrity in our society, we are in big trouble. Like it or not, lying is a part of being a child. Parents were not so trustworthy as teenagers either, and while we are at times devious as adults, most of us turned out not all that bad.

Lying *is* bad. I am not defending it. But it is also the normal response of the vast majority of teenagers either to cover up a wrong or to manipulate a situation in order to advance their cause.

But getting too caught up in the issue of lying can become a snare, leading to long harangues that go nowhere. The lies can take precedence over the problem at hand, namely, whatever the teenager did that was forbidden. Don't focus on the lying and lose sight of the more immediate and usually more important issues.

In the case of the boy who did not bring home the warning notices, the main problem was not that he lied, but that he was failing two subjects in school.

As for the girl who lied her way to an off-limits party, the main problem, well known to parents of teenage daughters, is trying to keep track of their daughters. The lying is assumed. And since parents cannot keep a teenage girl at home every night, they have to become especially adept at getting the facts as best they can *before* the crime is scheduled to take place.

"Wait a minute. You never mentioned before that Clarissa had an older brother who drives . . ."
"Yeah, well, it's not exactly her older brother. He's kind of like a good friend who she thinks of like a brother . . ."

Parents may feel that their daughters lie more than their sons, and this may well be the case. But there's a good reason for this. In general, boys do not have as great a need to sneak and lie because typically they are under much looser supervision and can get away with their ploy of providing no information at all. Many girls have to lie in order to even things out. It's the only recourse they have. Unfortunately, it can be rather draining on their parents.

How do parents actually make a difference in their child's becoming an honest person? The answer is actually simple: If parents are honest in dealing with others, especially in dealing with their own children, they are teaching honesty. If, on the other hand, they lie, especially with their own children, they are training them in dishonesty.

To tell a child to be honest is fine. To be mad at or to punish a child who lies is also fine. But parents should not delude themselves into thinking that these measures teach their children not to lie. They have meaning only when parents practice honesty.

"But I don't want my kid to grow up to be a liar. By not making a major issue of the lying, aren't I condoning it? Won't she then continue to be a liar as an adult?"

Not really. Lying as a teenager is not an especially reliable indicator of whether or not that teenager is, or will become, an honest person. A good part of teenage lying is a function of the strange amorality of the at-home self.

"Lying to my parents doesn't count. I really am an honest person."

Maybe so, but in any event the fact that a teenager lied to his parents indicates only that he lied to his parents. It does not mean he is on his way to a life of crime. It does not denote a moral crisis. We need to stay on top of what is going on as best as we can, but there is much we will not know about, much they will get away with. We should always confront them with their deceit when they are caught, and we must communicate our outrage. But a disaster, a tragedy, such deceit is not. Their sliminess may be deplorable, it is also normal, as it was with us when we were adolescents.

What's a parent to do? While it is good to trust one's children, it is also exceedingly foolish to do so in an area where they have already shown dishonesty. Trust should not be a blanket issue. Experience teaches us that it is appropriate to trust teenagers about some things and not about others. "I've found that I can trust Genevieve not to have boys over in the afternoon when no one is home. But we cannot trust her about what she says she is doing when she goes out weekend nights."

It is also a major mistake to feel that lying destroys a sacred trust. To be able to trust one's teenager is nice for parents, but more frequently it is a fool's paradise.

"You don't trust me."
"That's right. Am I supposed to?"
"But it's terrible you can't trust your own teenager."
"What's so terrible?"

5

Controlling Your
Teenager

You do not win the battle for control with teenagers. There are many things that parents absolutely do not want their teenage children to do—drink, use drugs, be sexually active, cut school, hang around with undesirable friends—but most teenagers do some or all of the above on a fairly regular basis. Many teenagers basically do what their parents want. Many more do not, not completely. And there is nothing that their parents can do to bring them under total control.

With adolescents, usually the best that you get is imperfect control. There are rules and they are obeyed, sometimes and sort of. Controlling teenagers is hard; often you don't win. Yet controls are absolutely necessary.

With the large majority of teenagers, this imperfect control is enough. It is all you need. It is not enough to save headaches and worries. Nothing can avoid that. But, for most teenagers, it will be quite sufficient to get through the adolescent years with both teenager and parent surviving in reasonably good shape.

The Parent Within

One source of parental control comes from a psychological fact of human development: the adolescent's parents are *already* a part of him, whether he likes it or not, as the teenager's own developing conscience. Therefore what parents say or do has clear entry into the teenager's head.

As discussed, what ends up as the independent adult conscience starts from the gradually internalized voice of the parents. By adolescence that voice, the conscience, is not yet completely the adolescent's own, nor is it wholly the separate real voice of the parents. It is somewhere in between, on the way to being the teenager's own independent conscience, but not there yet.

For the teenager this transition can be very frustrating and confusing. The teenager often hears the parents' voice in his or her own head and does not yet recognize that voice as his own. Teenagers hate the voice. They would like to strangle it, cast it out, get rid of it. But it will not go away, for it is already far too much a part of them. Later, when they are adults, the voice does fully become theirs, and, more often than not, they come to agree with their parents: "I should never have stayed out so late. What I got away with as a teenager!" And ultimately, as parents, they will make the same requirements of their own children, and pass down their own adult conscience, just as their parents did with them.

Establishing the Boundaries

It is a good idea to have rules.

"You have to be home on weekend nights by eleven."

"You may not have friends in the house after school when we are not here, unless it is Lisa Farrington."

"All of your dirty laundry should be put in the laundry hamper."

It is also okay for rules to be changed if, as I have discussed, it is the parent who sets the changes and is not bullied into them. It is even okay for teenagers to argue about a rule and convince their parents to change it. Rules can be in a constant state of flux.

"Okay, you can have Beverly Tesslington over after school too."

But there should always be rules. They do have power. They sit inside of the teenager's head and exert a constant pressure. And teenagers, though they would like to, can do nothing about these rules unless the parent abandons them. This is how, without recourse to threats or punishment, parents do exert a very real power over their children.

"You stayed out again last night way past your curfew. Do not think for a minute that that is acceptable. Two a.m. is way too late for you to be coming in. I want you in at eleven-thirty, and I expect you to be home on time in the future."

"I can come home when I want. Eleven-thirty is for babies. You can't stop me."

"That's right, I can't stop you. But the eleven-thirty curfew stays."

"I don't care."

But she does care. And the eleven-thirty curfew will continue to sit in her head exerting a steady pressure every time she goes out.

"Damn, my parents are such jerks. Eleven-thirty is ridiculous."

And with most children, more often than not, the curfew will pull them in on time. Teenagers choose to give their parents power over them because they do not like the alternative—too much hassling for not enough gains. The alternative would also mean that they would be truly free, truly responsible for themselves, and though any teenager would accept this leeway, we know it is not what they really want.

The conscious voice says, "Fuck you, asshole. Give me an apartment. Give me money. Give me a maid. I'm gonna do just fine. What responsibility? I'm gonna party."

Most teenagers, however, do not really desire such freedom. They have an investment in being good, more or less.

"I mean, it's not like I won't do shit. I drink, and I've smoked pot a few times. And there's been lots of times that I was places when my parents thought I was somewhere else. It's not like I'm good or anything. And there have been times that I've disobeyed my parents. But usually I don't, at least not that they get to know about it."

"Some of their rules really are stupid, and they do get me pissed off. But usually I can either figure a way around it, or if it's something that I really don't like, I make such a big fuss that I usually can get my parents to change their minds. But I wouldn't want to disobey them all of the time. What's the point?"

"I don't want to get into hassles with them. My life is okay. They're not ruining it. I don't want to do anything that's really going to upset the way things are. I just wish they'd get off my back a little more."

Most teenagers know that they have a pretty good deal. Teenagers do not want to disobey their parents. That is not their plan.

Teenagers do not want to overthrow the system of parental control, they just want to get around it.

What all this means is that parents of teenagers have considerably more power with their teenage children than they realize. There are some teenagers who will disobey and there is little that their parents can do to influence them. But with most, if parents confront their teenagers with each instance of disobedience, if they do not overreact to each transgression but keep their rules in place, they will have a teenager who obeys their rules, if imperfectly, and the rules, though tattered in places, will hold up.

Keeping the Rules in Place

"Jackie, you have to be home by eleven."

A rule is stated. This is the starting point for natural parent or stepparent or whoever is in charge. It is the main element of control. The rule must be there, in place, and it must be kept in place. Perhaps the teenager accepts the rule, at least initially, but perhaps she does not. Further discussion only leads to trouble. Maybe the child will obey. Maybe she will not. Getting into a fight with her to demand that she obey before she has actually disobeyed certainly sounds like a serious waste of energy.

In the face of a rule that they really do not like teenagers often have fits. Sometimes big fits. This is where the issue about separation comes in. If teenagers have fits because they are not getting their way, let them. The rule has been put in place. The best that a parent can do is to withdraw. This may not be easy, since teenagers not wanting to let go will try their hardest to pull the parent back in.

"I hate this house. I'm not going to do anything more that you ask me. I'm going to run away."

A parent must not respond. In fact, tantrums can often be good. It means that the parent has set a rule and stood by it, even though it is one that their child very much does not like. The essence of firm, strong parenting is the ability to make rules, unpopular though they may be, and keep them in place, regardless of the reaction that such rules may provoke. Now that the rule is firmly in place, the next step is up to the teenager.

Obeying the Spirit of the Law

It was a Saturday night. Vincent was supposed to be in by eleven-thirty. He got home at eleven-fifty. He got yelled at and was told that he had better be in by eleven-thirty the next time. He was not. In fact, he kept coming home anywhere from fifteen minutes to half an hour late. What's a parent to do?

The main thing a parent should do is realize that the curfew *is* working, though not perfectly. Vincent is not coming in punctually at eleven-thirty, but the eleven-thirty curfew is very definitely pulling him in. He is coming in late, but he is not coming in as if he had no curfew at all. He is not coming in whenever he feels like it, at 1 a.m., 2 a.m., or 7 a.m. after staying out all night at a friend's house, and without giving any notice.

"You mean I'm supposed to accept that he comes in late every time?"

At some level, yes. A parent should keep the eleven-thirty curfew in force and should react to every late appearance.

"Vincent, you are supposed to be home at eleven-thirty. Ten minutes of twelve is not eleven-thirty. You are going to have to come home at your curfew. You cannot continue coming in after it like you have been doing."

But how far should a parent go, how big should his weapons be, how much energy should he expend to enforce the letter of the law?

If grounding Vincent for coming in twenty minutes late gets him to obey the curfew more precisely, fine. But what if it does not? Or what if it works sometimes, but Vincent ends up being grounded almost every other weekend because he frequently comes in twenty minutes late. How much parental energy is appropriate to try to get a teenage boy to come in precisely when he is told? I think the answer is some energy, but not a lot.

After all, adolescents can differentiate between the spirit (the intent) and the letter of a law. And often they will obey the intent of a rule; but maddeningly, and at times even intentionally so, just to show they are independent, they will not obey *exactly*. Parents must realize that their rules are working, just not perfectly.

Devious Defiance

Once rules are established, teenagers try to avoid flagrant disobedience. The majority of teenagers will shy away from direct defiance. Normally there is a line that most of them would rather not cross. They prefer to be devious. This is when their lying is at its best. Teenagers do not mind disobeying, they just do not want their parents to know about it.

"Yeah. If they don't know about it, what's the problem?"

"I don't know. I don't hate my parents. I just don't like any of their rules. But I don't think I have the nerve just to say no to all their rules and then do what I want. I'd be afraid they'd kick me out. Even if they didn't, it would be too weird. Christine Landauer does that with her parents, and everybody knows she's crazy."

Therefore most teenage disobedience lies in the realm of sleaze and deception. When confronted by a rule they do not like teenagers will do all they can to get it changed, to somehow get around it, to confuse the issue, or, where they feel they can safely contrive not to get caught, to disobey the rule altogether. They will tell half-truths, lies, whatever is necessary to accomplish their objective. They are not above enlisting friends as aides in their deviousness:

"Around seven tonight call my house, and if either of my parents answers, say that you don't need to speak to me, but ask them to tell me that you need my history book tonight. Okay?"

The teenage preference for deviousness over open defiance is an important fact for parents to keep in mind. It dictates their strategy. The primary rule in trying to combat teenage deception is that any rule must be as explicitly stated as possible.

"Mom, I'm going over to Yvonne's after school. Can I call you to pick me up around six?"
"All right, dear."

Later that evening:

"Pick you up where? I've never heard of her. I thought you said you were going to be at Yvonne's."

"Yeah, I was. But then we went over to Rochelle's. Is there any problem with that?"

If the mother wants her daughter to stay at Yvonne's, she had better state it. "All right, you may go to Yvonne's but I don't want you going anywhere else unless you call and ask."

"Mom, me and Yvonne are over at Rochelle's, is that okay?"
"I meant for you to call me before you went anywhere."
"Oh, sorry, Mom. I didn't understand."

They can be pretty slimy.
"But I can't anticipate everything she's going to do. She's so good at thinking of new ways to twist what I said. Each time it's something different."
It can be difficult. Parents can only learn through experience, but they can learn and they had better learn if they want a reasonable degree of control over their teenage children.

"Okay. Mrs. Porfirio is driving you to the movies. But how are you getting back? . . . Lana's brother? I don't remember that Lana had a brother. How old is Lana's brother?"

The more clear you are in the beginning, the more you can pin them down, the better the control you will exert. The less room they have in which to maneuver and disobey, the less likely that they will. Also, if a parent is very clear about precisely what a teenager is allowed to do, then if he does disobey, he can better be confronted with his disobedience without as much risk of his sliding off the hook. Confronting teenagers when they have disobeyed is very important. Confrontations can often be defused by glib teenagers when initial instructions were not adequately clear.

"But I couldn't call you to ask whether it was okay to go out after the movies because there wasn't time. Everybody was leaving and I didn't want to get stranded."

"No, Ricky. I said that if you go anywhere after the movies you must call and let me know, and that you have to call from the theater. I had asked you if they have phones there, and you said, 'Yes.' There is no excuse. I asked you to call, and you didn't."

Direct Disobedience

It was Friday night and Elisha was supposed to be home by eleven-thirty. She did not get home until after one. She had not called, and what excuses she offered were flimsy at best.

"We had to take Cheryl home first and we lost track of time."

Clearly Elisha had not wanted to come home at eleven-thirty and had not tried to. She had flatly disobeyed her parents' rule. What should a parent do?

Confrontation is the beginning and the end of what parents should do when faced with blatant disobedience.

One a.m., however, is not the best time for confrontations. Such after-hours episodes can often yield regrettable results. One a.m. is time for going to sleep. The next morning usually serves better.

"Elisha, come down here. I want to talk to you."
"What?"
"I said, Elisha, come downstairs."
"Okay. What?"
"You came in after one o'clock last night and you were supposed to be in at eleven-thirty. I don't care who else was supposed to be driven home, you knew you had to be home at

eleven-thirty. It is your responsibility to keep track of the time. You may not stay out that late. There is no excuse."

"Eleven-thirty's too early."

"We've been over all that before. Eleven-thirty is your curfew on Friday nights and it's not going to change."

"You can't make me come in if I don't want to."

"Eleven-thirty is your curfew and what you did last night is not okay."

"You treat me like I was in junior high."

As discussed repeatedly, the parent, having made his or her point, should now say no more. Any future discussion is counterproductive. This is confrontation.

Confrontation has three parts:

1. A clear statement that the rule has been broken
2. Emphasis that such behavior is not acceptable
3. A declaration that the rule remains in effect

This confrontation is the core of parental control of teenagers. Really, parents have little more. It's an effective method, but it only works with those teenagers who ultimately do buy into the system of control, who ultimately do not want to rock the boat, at least not too much. And this is most teenagers. With most of them, the system works.

More or less extraneous to the whole situation are threats, groundings, physical punishment, lectures on motivation and attitude, and even rewards. These means might have some effect, but not usually. They mean little because of two basic facts about the control of teenagers.

The first fact is that the only way to truly control a teenager, or anyone else, is to physically stop them. With small children that is exactly what we do.

"No, Clarissa, don't put your tongue in that light socket."

And we go over and pick up Clarissa and pull her away from the light socket.

Unfortunately, with teenagers it gets a little more difficult.

"No, Clarissa, you may not smoke marijuana."

I have envisioned parents who really want full-time control of their teenage children hiring a fast ex-football player. His job would be to trail the kid around and intervene whenever a rule was broken.

"No, Clarissa, put down that joint"—he physically grabs the marijuana cigarette.

"Get the fuck out of my face. I can't believe my parents actually hired you. You're ruining my life, you stupid prick."

There are, in fact, programs that basically follow the above model. These are twenty-four-hour tracking programs in which workers are assigned to shadow youthful offenders. In some communities they are an alternative to incarceration. I hope it goes without saying that this method is impractical and, more important, inappropriate for most families. It's ridiculous to even consider it.

The second fact is that no threat, punishment, or reward will have any effect whatsoever *unless the child himself buys into the system*. The best illustration is this classic "you break the rule, you suffer the consequences" scenario:

"Elisha, you came home at one. You were supposed to be in at eleven-thirty. Now you have to take the consequences of your disobedience. You are grounded for a week."

Simple. Clean. Faultless in construction. But the fact remains that in order for such a system to work, Elisha must buy into it. That is, though she may bitch and moan at the grounding, rail at the incredible unfairness of her parents, fuss at how they treat her like a baby and give her no freedom, it is *she and she alone* who empowers the system. Unless her parents were to actually lock her in the house and hire the football player to keep her in, Elisha could leave if she wanted to. All she has to do to destroy the effectiveness of the grounding as a control is to walk out the door.

The fact is, if teenagers choose to absolutely violate their parents' rules, they can.

Parents' Greatest Error

The greatest error that parents of teenagers can make is to believe that disobedience means total loss of control. Believing this, they often go all out, sometimes with dire consequences, to reestablish the control that they have not really lost to begin with. Escalating punishments ultimately run out, and all that is left is chaos.

"I can't stand this. They won't let me do anything. Fuck them. I don't care what they do to me. What else can they do anyway?"

With *any* teenager on a given evening the lure of being with friends, being a part of what is going on, may be just too strong to resist. In the choice between obeying parents' rules and not missing out on fun with friends, parents' rules will lose out. Most teenagers will disobey in certain situations, regardless of the consequences.

What can parents do to control their teenage children? They must make rules and they must continually confront their children when these rules are broken. And if broken, the rules should nonetheless be kept in place. Teenagers will disobey again. There is nothing that will totally stop them. And there are some teenagers who will disobey continually no matter what one does. Confrontation is an effective control, but it only works, as will anything, with those who ultimately do buy into the system of control.

Out of Control

What of the children who go beyond the acceptable? What of those who truly ignore the rules, come and go when they please, and perhaps use drugs, do serious drinking, and hang out with friends who are clearly up to no good? What can the parents do with the teenager who refuses to do anything around the house and does badly in school, cutting classes or whole days regularly?

These are the times when parents often employ "get tough" approaches. They may try to enlist the courts or the social service system. Some parents may say to the adolescent, "Live here by our rules, or don't live here at all," and they will lock their child out of their house, sometimes making sure there are alternative living arrangements, but sometimes not. These measures may sometimes shock teenagers into better behavior, but often if there is any change in behavior, it is only temporary.

Parents who seek help through the courts or the social service system often find that unless their child actually has criminal charges pending for car theft, breaking and entering, drug sales, or the like, there is not much that these systems can do.

The proverbial foster home is rarely an option. These homes tend to be available only to children who have no viable home to live in. Where there is a viable home, when physical or sexual abuse is not an ongoing risk, foster homes, always at a premium, are rarely used for disobedient teenagers.

Sometimes parents enlist the help of mental health professionals. And this can prove beneficial. It may mean calling up a local mental health clinic. Or parents can ask friends or a family doctor for the names of counselors who work with teenagers and their families. I have always been surprised by how teenagers, perhaps contrary to what one might expect, seem to like professional counseling. Sometimes family problems that are causing difficulties can be worked through. Teenagers can listen and talk to a counselor in a way that they could never tolerate with their parents. But sometimes, even with the most enlightened of professional help, teenagers remain out of control.

What options are left? Very few. Parents in these situations are stuck with a teenager living at home over whom they basically have no control. He or she simply has not bought into *any* system of control, and is not likely to.

I have asked myself what I would do if confronted with the above situation. I am not sure, but I prefer to think I would hang in as best as I could. Hopefully I would follow my own advice and keep my rules in place despite the fact that my son or daughter was constantly disobeying them.

"You came in again at three-thirty. We don't want you out that late."
"Fuck you, Dad."

And I hope I would emphasize that my concern was not about their disobedience but about their welfare.

"I worry about you. I don't want anything bad to happen to you. I know you think that you know what you're doing. But I don't think so, and I do worry."
"Right."

Parents of such children must endure and they must wait. In time, one of two things will come to happen. Their child may mature and the period of flagrant disobedience may come to an end even as their increased age allows them more freedom. Or they may remain awful, unrepentant, doing as they please, and for the most part unpleasant to be around. Parents now have a choice because these children are no longer "children." Parents are free to allow them to remain in the home or not. And often, though it turns out to be not so easy to kick a "child" out of the house, this is exactly what some parents must do.

6

Conflict

Conflict is the meat and potatoes of most parent-teenager relationships. The fact is, most interaction between parent and teenager involves some form of conflict.

"That's the truth. I'm either yelling at him for something he was or wasn't supposed to do, or I'm yelling at him because I didn't like his tone of voice. He only talks to me when he wants something."

It does seem this way. To have no conflict at all is to have either a parent who does not care or a child who is visiting his aunt in Florida. Of course, the reason for so much conflict is that we make requirements of teenagers—take out the trash, clean rooms, get up on time in the morning, be home by a particular time—and very often they don't do it.

"But there is so much conflict and so little of anything nice."

Yes, but conflict is not necessarily bad. Remember that always lurking beneath the surface with an adolescent, waiting to make trouble, is the pull not to separate from the parent, not to move forward, not to grow up. This temptation is especially true at times of limit setting, and an excellent way to cling is to battle. This is why conflict so often seems to get out of hand and take on a life of its own, far beyond where the conflict had begun, far beyond what it's worth. Parents must see these wars for what they truly are—desperate measures on the part of the child's baby self *not to let go*.

The art of parenting lies in recognizing this dynamic of adolescence and learning how to avoid playing unwittingly into its grasp. The secret to a good outcome lies not in a final resolution—there never will be one if the teenager can help it—but in ending the discussion and walking away. Therefore the following discussion is not about avoiding conflict, but rather about limiting conflict to what is useful and necessary, avoiding battles that are tumultuous, draining, and disheartening.

Battles (and What to Do about Them in General)

Battles are both the essence and the supreme test of being the parent of a teenager. Battles can lead to physical harm. They can cause children to run away or to attempt suicide. Battles can create permanent rifts. They can lead parents to divorce. Nevertheless, battles can also mean nothing and can be totally forgotten—by the teenager—within minutes.

A battle begins:

"*I want to stay out until one o'clock tonight. Everybody else is allowed to.*"
"*No, Emily.*"

"*Justin, take out the trash.*"
"*I can't. My arm hurts. And besides, Becky's supposed to.*"

In both cases the parent wants one thing, and the child wants something else. The child is being asked to do what he does not want to do. More basically, he or she is being asked to accept a loss—not getting his or her way. A loss means accepting bad feelings and this is a signal for action to the ever-present baby self lurking just below the surface, the self that wants only fun, no stress. It decides to make an appearance, thinking:

Emily: "I don't feel like being disappointed about not being allowed to stay out until one o'clock."

Justin: "I don't feel like straining myself to lift up the trash basket and carry it all the way out to the garage. What I feel like is getting my way. Then I won't have to have any bad feelings. Yuck! I hate bad feelings."

And so the teenager digs in for battle.

Emily: "What do you mean, 'No'? You're crazy. I'm gonna stay out until one and I don't care what you say. You can't do anything to stop me."

Justin: "I'm not gonna take the trash. It's Becky's turn. It's just not fair. I'm always the one who has to do stuff."

This is the crucial part of a battle. It comes very early in the sequence of events. The parents have clearly stated their intention; the children, their defiance. The stage is set for a battle of wills. It is *now*, immediately, that parents must end their participation. To continue is to be sucked into a trap that inevitably causes matters to go one way—downhill.

The parent can have one last line, but one line only:

"*Emily, you are to be home by eleven-thirty.*"

"*Justin, take out the trash, now!*"

They need say no more. Their children, on the other hand, are just beginning.

Emily: "*I'm not going to be home by eleven-thirty. You can't make me. I'm fifteen, I'm not a baby. You're totally unreasonable. You are. And I'm not going to do what you say. I mean it. You're such a bitch.*"

Justin: "*Becky gets everything she wants. All you want me for is somebody to do chores. I don't even know if you like me. Maybe I'd be better off living somewhere else. I don't know if you'd miss me.*"

These two teenage responses are of course readily identifiable as Tactic 7A—threat of absolute disobedience with accompanying profanity—and Tactic 13B—complaint of unfairness, switching over to grief at feeling unloved. Both tactics plead for parental response. But parents must not respond. If they do, all is lost.

"You listen to me. You will be home by eleven-thirty or face the consequences." Or perhaps picking up on the name-calling: "Don't you dare call me a bitch."

Or, as with Justin's parent: "I don't know how you can say things like that. That's ridiculous. We certainly do not favor Becky over you."

Now the parent has gone one step too far. She has fallen into the trap. Teenagers can easily keep the responses coming.

Emily: "*I don't care about consequences. Ground me for a year. That's all you know how to do.*"
Or: "*I will too dare call you a bitch. Bitch.*"

Justin: "*You don't realize it, but you really do favor Becky. You're not even aware of how much you let her get away with.*"

Teenagers do not consciously plan to keep the battles going. It just comes out: the ever-present voice of the baby inside who does not want to let go. For if the argument ends, the baby is alone. And its influence starts to fade. If alone, with no parent to fight with, the child's debate becomes internal.

Emily: "*Shit. I really do want to stay out until one o'clock. If I leave early, I'm gonna miss stuff. But I don't know if I really want to chance breaking my curfew by that much. I might get into more trouble than it's worth. Shit. I don't know what to do.*"

Internal conflict. Stress. These feelings are part of the independent mode of functioning and will emerge if the girl cannot keep the fight going.

Justin: "*I hate taking out the trash. It's such a drag. I know I should do it, but I hate it.*"

An internal struggle ensues between his conscience, which knows he should do it, and his laziness. But if he can keep the scene going, he never has to deal with this conflict— conscience versus laziness—which is precisely the conflict that a parent wants him to have to face.

Parents must not allow themselves to get sucked into ongoing battles. It is that simple. They must keep focused on the issue at hand, state a position, and carry it no further. To do so is to invite chaos.

It is not unusual for parents to lock themselves in a bathroom to escape children who persist in arguing. But the biggest obstacle to letting matters rest is not persistent teenagers, but persistent parents. Adolescents are very good at knowing what gets to their parents. They well know how to keep their parents going.

"I can't let her get away with saying *that*."

"But he really seems upset. I can't just leave it like this."

But you must. There is one immutable fact of child raising: as long as children can stay in contact with their parents, even through arguing, they do not have to go off on their own. Understanding this prime fact will save enormous wear and tear; ignoring it is to ask for trouble.

Many Doors to Doom

They trap us, with each technique more artful than the last. In truth, their methods are not preconceived but are spontaneous urgings of their hearts, unconsciously but unerringly designed especially for us, drawing on their wisdom from all the years together. Their words are all the more beguiling, all the more effective, because of their conviction. Lie detectors would show that teenagers believe what they say.

Here are a few of the most common "traps." But no list could possibly enumerate the unique set of such traps custom-tailored to fit each parent's particular vulnerabilities. What follows is a mere sampling of some of the most tried and true.

Teenagers' Traps for Parents

"I Don't Care"

This trap is particularly effective, as it seems to pull the rug out from under parents.

"Stephanie, I am sick and tired of your thinking that you can do whatever you want. You can just forget about going out for the next two weekends."

"I don't care."

This sign-off begs this response:

"You don't care, well, we'll see what you care about . . ."

The parent, feeling powerless, now seeks greater leverage. The teenager continues with more of the same.

"You can do anything you want. But I don't care."

The parent, feeling that she has to come up with something that will have an effect, keeps going. A full-scale battle inevitably results. Which is just what the baby inside the teenager was looking for.

The trick is that adolescents do care. They are just saying that they don't. The correct response to "I don't care" is no response at all.

"Yes, I will"
This technique and its companion, "No, I won't," are much beloved by every generation of teenagers and have reduced many a parent to the level of a two-year-old.

"Charlene, you may not go to the mall after school tomorrow."
"I will too."
"Charlene, you heard what I said."
"I will too go."
"I am warning you, Charlene."
"You can't stop me. What are you going to do, come home from work?"
"Don't try me, Charlene."

The trick here is that children risk nothing by *saying* that they will defy their parents' orders. They may have no intention of disobeying, but lose nothing by asserting that they will. In addition, they may even succeed in picking a fight. And then they will certainly carry the battle for all it's worth.

"I'm going to go to the mall, Mom. I really mean it."

Having already stated their position, parents need say no more. They should deal with disobedience *only* when and if it happens. They should ignore all mere threats of disobedience.

"You're an Asshole"
This is a particular winner. All a child has to do is direct a verbal attack at a parent—swearing is especially good, though not always necessary for the creative child—and the parent resumes a fight that had been concluded.

"That's it, Patrick, I am not giving you money for the jacket. I have nothing more to say."
"You're an asshole."
"What did you say? Get over here. Don't you dare swear at me."

And the parent has reentered the argument. Parents may feel that a particular remark has gone too far, and I will not question their judgment, but parents must also realize that picking up on teenage jabs risks undoing what may have just been accomplished.

"I Can't Do Anything Right"
This example is more subtle than the others, but equally devastating.

"Get down here and take out the trash now. I am sick and tired of always having to get after you. When are you going to learn a little responsibility? When are you going to grow up?"
"You're always criticizing me. I can't ever please you. I'm just a failure, aren't I?"

If picked up on, this can turn the whole scenario into much more pleasing directions for the teenager, because the subject is no longer the nasty trash that needs to be taken out.

"You're not a failure, Andy. How can you say things like that? You're not a failure, it's just that we sometimes get mad that we have to keep after you to do things."

"That's not true, you and Mom are disappointed in me. You wish I was different."

This is a particularly insidious ploy, for both parent and child. Its effectiveness lies in the ability of the child to pull out of himself feelings of sadness and lack of worth which, if they are to be well played, must be believed. And many children *can* lock into a sadness that has no origin other than the effect that it produces in their parents.

In fact, many children maintain a tie with their parents through sadness. They learn quite early that being sad or upset can get attention of a special and pleasing sort. Over time, repeatedly using this ploy, they come to believe it.

"But lots of teenagers *are* sad. I don't want to ignore him if he says he feels worthless. What if he went on to kill himself after I had ignored him?"

The key to parental response is to consider the context of such statements. If you're uncertain, pick a neutral time and ask, "Andy, do you really feel you're a failure? Do you really feel that we think that you are?" An affirmative answer at that time should be taken seriously. But if the answer is no, parents can safely discount those times when Andy's "depression" coincides with asking him to take out the trash.

There are many doors to doom, and some lie within parents themselves. The baby self that does not want to let go exists within every parent too. Once the fight begins it is not always so easy for parents to let go either. But they simply *must*, because they are the adults.

How Parents Trap Themselves

However, distinct from anything that teenagers may do, there are certain serious traps that lurk within the minds of parents. Traps that can ensnare them in fruitless—even destructive—battles with their teenage children.

Correcting Character Flaws

Probably the most common and most insidious trap is one that makes parents feel that they cannot let a matter drop because their child's very character is at stake.

It was a Sunday and it snowed. Jerry shoveled the walk and the driveway. Later that day it snowed a little more, stopping around mid-evening. Jerry was in his room lying on his bed listening to music. His father asked him to clear off the walk and the driveway again. The job would probably take about twenty minutes, no more.

"*Dad, I already did it. The new snow is nothing. It doesn't need to be shoveled.*"

"*Jerry, it needs to be done. If it's not shoveled you know how it turns to ice.*"

"*Dad, it doesn't need to be done.*"

"*Jerry, go outside and clear off the snow now.*"

"*No, it doesn't need it. If you want it done so much, I don't see why you can't do it yourself.*"

No matter how you could look at it, no explanations other than bad ones exist for Jerry's behavior. He was lazy and obnoxious.

But this is not an unusual situation. Teenagers often act in ways that are uncompromisingly grotesque. In these situations parents frequently make what is probably the major and most common error in dealing with their teenage children, an error based on faulty assumptions that go to the heart of being the parent of a teenager.

"He's so lazy. If I can't make him change now, when is he ever going to change? I can't let him get away with this behavior. I only have a few years left before he's going to be gone. It's my responsibility to shape him up before it's too late."

"Jerry, you lazy jerk. What the hell do you think you're doing? You just lie on your bed all day and listen to music. You can't even do a simple job when I ask you."

"That's not fair, Dad. I do do stuff. I'd do more if you didn't yell at me so much."

"I yell at you because you don't do anything. I can't believe you're so lazy. What are you going to do when you're older? Do you think you're always going to find somebody to wait on you? I pity your wife. So help me God, you better learn to straighten yourself out."

Jerry rises from his bed and leaves the room. "I'm getting the fuck out of here. You clean up your own fucking driveway."

"Don't you dare swear at me. You come back here."

What was Jerry's father's error? He believed that since his child demonstrated major character flaws (rudeness, laziness), he himself had to act to correct those flaws, especially since there was so little time left before Jerry would be on his own and no longer under parental influence. The faulty assumptions were, first, that his intervention would even have any effect and, second, that the character flaws so clearly revealed in the snow-shoveling episode were destined to be part of his child's character as an adult.

The fact is, if a teenager is destined to grow up to be a jerk, parental interventions are not going to do much to change that. Parents who try very hard to prevent warped character development in an obnoxious teenager are usually wasting their time. They are fighting a battle *that they have already won or lost*. They just don't realize it.

However, Jerry's father compounded his first error with another error. In his attempt to change a character flaw in his son he was compelled to lecture Jerry on the consequences of laziness rather than sticking to the issue of the conflict—was Jerry going to shovel the driveway? Teenagers will often use a lecture as an excuse for not doing something. In this case, the lecture achieved the opposite of what was intended. It allowed Jerry to avoid confronting his laziness.

Lectures do very little. They can play into the hands of the adolescent who doesn't want to separate from the parents. A lecture allows Jerry to stay attached by fussing, rather than having to deal with the question of whether he should shovel the snow again.

Parents can rave at their children. They can pull out all the stops in order to change pernicious characteristics. But their energy will be wasted and they will succeed only in producing longer, nastier scenes. Any overall effect will be to slow down the process of maturing.

Only one good reason exists to rave at one's child: it makes *us* feel better. We should not delude ourselves as to who it is that benefits from our lectures.

"Well. I certainly gave it to him that time."

"Dad is such a jerk. I hate it when he talks like this. Why can't he just leave me alone? I really would do a whole lot better if he didn't bitch at me so much. I'm not lazy. I would do it if he'd just back off and not treat me like a little kid. He

thinks that because I'm his son he has the right to yell at me. I'm not going to do stuff for him when he comes on like such a prick."

Jerry's father would have been better off insisting on his original request and not getting sidetracked with son-improvement lectures.

"Jerry, shovel the driveway."
"No, it doesn't need it. Get off my back."
"Jerry. Shovel the driveway. I don't want to have to shovel it. I want you to shovel it. Now."
"No. It doesn't need it."
"Jerry, I want you to shovel the driveway."

And if the scene is played this way, with Jerry's father avoiding lectures but staying with his demand, Jerry usually will go out and sullenly shovel the walk. Usually, simply staying with a specific demand will achieve its aim.

Just Drop It
Getting even. Getting in the last word. Not letting them get away with it. Teaching them a lesson. In the realm of child raising, these measures almost assure disaster. Can't we just drop it? Leave it there? End it? We're adults, after all. But apparently this is very difficult.

"Simone, where is my white sweater?"
"Umm. It's in my room."
"I thought I told you that I did not want you wearing it."
"I forgot."
"How dare you keep taking my clothes without my permission!"

"*Mom, I didn't have anything to wear. Rochelle had borrowed my green sweater.*"

"*What are you doing lending your clothes to your friends all the time and then you don't have anything to wear and you take my clothes?*"

"*Why are you always yelling at me? I hate you.*"

"*Don't you dare talk to me that way. Don't you use that tone of voice.*"

"*I'll use whatever tone of voice I want.*"

"*Don't you talk back to me.*"

And on and on.
Why not:

"*Simone, where is my white sweater?*"
"*Umm. It's in my room.*"
"*Thanks.*"

Or if that's too hard:

"*Thank you, Simone. But please don't use my white sweater again. I asked you not to before.*"
"*I forgot.*"

Finis.

We can always give a million reasons why we should not drop it. And usually these reasons sound more or less reasonable. Typically they involve "not letting them just get away with it" or "teaching them . . ." or "making sure they learn . . ."

But if our aim is not to get caught up in lengthy battles, if our aim is to have them learn something positive, then, almost invariably, the greatest wisdom is simply to shut up. By going on, we teach them only one thing: we want to be in control.

And the scene invariably switches from the issue at hand to a battle of wills.

There are, of course, still other traps that can pull parents unwittingly into battles. Many of these involve other family members. Siblings, three-way mother-father-teenager altercations. They will be discussed shortly in the section about families.

How Can You Ask Me to Take You to the Mall After What Just Happened Fifteen Minutes Ago?

Even where parents have the best intentions, battles do occur, and if not usually physical, they nonetheless can get pretty nasty. What may be most perplexing and infuriating to parents is how quickly their teenagers seem to recover from such battles. Whereas they themselves are still emotionally exhausted, their children seem to have totally forgotten about what had just transpired only minutes before.

Valerie was supposed to wash all of the linen napkins. Her mother would pick them up after work and bring them to a woman who would dye them purple. Valerie remembered the task when she got home from school but kept putting it off, instead watching TV and calling a friend. She had not meant *not* to wash the napkins, but she had not really meant to wash them either.

When Valerie's mother came home to find that Valerie had done nothing, she became angry. Despite knowing she was in the wrong, Valerie defended herself by saying that it was unreasonable for her mother to assign her tasks in the afternoon, because school is long and hard, and it was not fair to make such demands on her. She had a right to relax after school.

This only infuriated Valerie's mother further, and the scene then degenerated into screaming on both sides.

"You are the most inconsiderate, selfish girl in the world. You make me ashamed. What did I do wrong?"

"I hate you and I hate Daddy and I hate this house. I can't wait to get out of here. If you think I'm gonna stay here another two years, you're crazy. I can't stand you. I hate you."

Whereupon Valerie ran to her room sobbing and slammed the door. Valerie's mother was upset, but nevertheless prepared supper although she continued to feel shaken. Thirty minutes later Valerie emerged from her room and entered the family room, where her mother, still upset, was reading the newspaper.

"Mom, could you drop me off at the mall after supper? I can meet Yvette there and get a lift home from her mother."
"What?"
"I said, 'Can you give me a ride to the mall?' "
"What?"
"I said, 'Can you give me a ride to the mall?' "
"I don't believe you. How can you come in here and act like nothing happened? How can you dare to ask me to take you to the mall, especially after what you said to me?"
"Oh, that."

It is a major issue for parents of adolescents. The general principle demonstrated in this dialogue is that from an adolescent's standpoint, most issues are of the moment. They may not be from their parents' standpoint, but they are from the adolescent's. And although teenagers may feel that they mean what they say at the time, they really don't.

"*Do you really hate your mother?*"

"*No. But I do when she acts like a jerk.*"

"*Do you hate your father?*"

"*No. I just said that because it sounded good at the time.*"

"*Do you want to leave your parents' house before you finish high school?*"

"*No, not really. Where would I go? I mean, they do get to me sometimes. But I like my room. And besides, I know my parents aren't that bad. They're just parents.*"

"*Don't you care that you say such terrible things to your mother?*"

"*No. She knows I don't mean it. Besides, she shouldn't have said what she said. She's not perfect either, you know.*"

Like it or not, teenagers, especially teenage girls, can become very upset, get very nasty, and get over it very fast. What they say in the heat of battle can mean nothing other than that they are mad. Half an hour after a major blowup, Valerie can ask her mother to take her to the mall, not because she's being sweet and manipulative but because she genuinely feels that the fight that happened a half hour ago is finished. Her mother got mad at her for something she failed to do, and she got mad at her mother for yelling at her. And now it's over.

A parent may wish she could say to a child, "It's not over. You cannot expect to act that way and then come back as if nothing happened. You may not talk to me the way you did. You are going to have to learn that what you do and say has consequences."

The parent may say this and may indeed punish a child for disrespect. What punishment accomplishes, as anybody who has been through this will attest, is nothing. Nothing positive, that is. The same thing will happen again anyway. The speech is effective only in assuring that the fight resumes.

From the parent's standpoint, the underlying issue in these episodes, once again, is that most difficult of all parenting skills—letting go.

Beyond Words

Unfortunately, sometimes parents, rather than pulling back, can get very angry indeed. Angry enough to hit. Many parents use spanking as punishment with younger children. Many parents spontaneously smack their children when they get mad at them. Is this ever okay? It is an issue open to debate. But there is no debate in regard to hitting teenagers. It should not be done.

Teenagers experience hitting, any hitting, quite differently from preadolescents. To them it is a physical, even sexualized, insult. Remember that two main psychological features of adolescence are the upswing in sexuality and the mandate to feel independent from one's parents. With adolescence, physical intimacy with one's parents must therefore be sealed off; distinct boundaries now exist between parent and child, and being hit is experienced as a violation of those boundaries. Adolescents react so strongly to hitting that the act is simply unacceptable. In response to a blow, teenagers can become violently upset, so upset that they can do harm to themselves or others. Whether they deserve it or not, one must back off. Regardless of how one feels about hitting younger children, the cardinal rule about teenagers is that one must not hit them.

To complicate matters, teenagers sometimes hit their parents. This too has a different meaning from when they were younger. There should now be a strong taboo against such behavior inside them. By hitting their parents, teenagers indicate they are seriously out of control. At that point, invariably, parents must seek immediate outside help, possibly even from the police. Teenagers are not little kids, and the act of hitting has the potential of real harm.

Jobs Around the House

Coming in when they are supposed to is probably the cause of the most serious parent-teenage battles. But unquestionably jobs around the house that are not getting done most commonly cause fights. This section is about the latter category. Dirty glasses left sitting in the family room, overflowing trash cans, requested chores that get put off forever—these seem to be the topic of most conversations.

"That's right. I don't have regular conversations. Most of my time that I spend with Darren seems to be me fussing at him about something. But what can I do? He simply won't cooperate."

"Darren, are these your socks?"
"Yeah. So what?"

Of course, there are teenagers who do chores regularly, without hassle. But many do not. It is just not possible to get them to do all that's asked. Further, what one does get is often accompanied by objections. Many teenagers can be so caught up in their own immediate wants and needs that they will go through periods in which they will regularly ignore chores around the home, feel only hassled by their parents, expect their parents to do everything for them, and not see that they are doing anything wrong. It remains necessary to stay on top of them all the time.

Years ago teenagers did more around the house than they do today, and with less objection, mainly because parents used harsher controls. But also, with the major increase in labor-saving devices over the years, the need for help around the house has significantly decreased. The fact is, teenagers respond much better to *need* than to what they see as obligation. Teenagers will more readily get up early in the morning to milk the cows, if otherwise the cows will not get milked, than they will move dirty glasses from one room to another.

"You don't understand. I have my life and there are things that are important to me. And bringing dishes into the kitchen just is not one of them. If it's so important to her, why can't she just do it herself without bugging me about it? She knows how much I hate to do it. Besides, she's always asking me when I'm doing something else. Talking on the phone to one's best friend may not seem very important to her, but it is to me. It's very important. Glasses going into the kitchen is not very important to me. She just doesn't remember what it was like when she was my age. They had phones then too. I'll bet she wasn't so perfect."

And to say that the problem is that kids today are just too lazy is missing the point. Most teenagers, as their confused parents well know, can be incomprehensibly lazy at home but also be a hard worker at an after-school job. The reason, of course, is that issue of the "home" and the "away from home" selves in operation. Knowing this still does not help much when the simplest jobs go begging.

To Nag or Not to Nag

"I don't want to be always nagging him. But if I don't, then he won't do anything."

"I try never to be in the same room as her. Anytime she comes to where I am, or I go through where she is, she always wants me to do something. I'm not kidding—every time. As

soon as I hear her getting near me, I start to get tense. What is she going to fuss at me about now?"

"See? That's just what I'm afraid of. I want us to have a nice relationship, but all he sees me as is a nag, because that's all I ever seem to do."

"Yeah. Right. I got an idea, why don't you stop nagging me about stuff? You'd see. We'd really get along a lot better."

"Yes, that's what I want. But you'd never pick up, and you'd never do anything you're supposed to do."

"So? That's no big deal, and we'd really be happier."

"You mean if you leave plates with half-eaten sandwiches in the middle of the rug, I shouldn't say anything?"

"Yeah. Try it. I'll pick it up after a while, or you can pick it up."

"I can't do it. It's too obscene. I can't let him. I mean, his room is one thing, but I just can't let him not do anything. But I don't want to be a nag. I think there are times that he really hates me."

"It's true. There's a lot of the time where she's really the biggest pain in my life. I mean, maybe it's a terrible thing to say, but I'd be happier if she simply wasn't around."

"I knew it. I knew he felt that way."

An absolute fact of adolescence is that if you do not nag, they will not do what you want. They may not do it even if you do nag. If having a teenager do nothing is acceptable to you, then do not nag. But if it is not, you are stuck with nagging.

"There has to be something else."

What?

"You mean if I want him to do stuff, I'm going to have to nag?"

That's right.

"Then I guess I have to keep nagging."

"I'm going to hate you forever if you nag. It will sour our whole relationship throughout my adolescence."

"Tough."

I'll Do It Later

If a parent wants something done, he had better make his child do it right away. Otherwise, the odds are it will not get done, and the parent will get very irritated.

"Andre, will you empty the litter box?"
"Yeah, sure. In a little while, okay?"

"Andre, you said you were going to take out the litter box."
"Yeah, Mom, I will. Don't worry."
"When?"
"I will. Soon."

"Andre, I asked you to take out the litter box early this afternoon, and I have kept reminding you. I am sick and tired of always having to tell you to do things. You should do it without my even having to ask you."
"I'm sorry, Mom. I forgot."
"You forgot? You forgot? When are you going to grow up?"

A better way:

"Andre, will you empty the litter box?"
"Yeah, sure. In a little while, okay?"
"No. Do it now."
"I will, in a while."
"No. Now!"

"No. I'm in the middle of doing something. Besides, you don't have to yell."

"Andre! Now!"

"All right. But you don't have to always yell at me."

It is the only way.

If She Won't Do for Me . . .

With the new teenager chores may not get done, at least not without a hassle. And in response, parents do get angry and, not unjustifiably, may feel taken advantage of.

"She is going to have to do her chores without my nagging her all of the time—or she's going to be sorry. I'll take things away. Privileges. Or maybe I just won't do anything for her. She won't do what I want. I won't do what she wants. Next time Helene wants a ride to the mall, let's see what happens. That would teach her that the world is not just give, give, give."

There is an important line here. Let us say that my child has just done something that really makes me mad. I was trying to straighten up the living room, asked for his help, and all he did was to give me a hard time. As a result, I am mad at him. If he then asks me to take him to the mall—not something which had been previously planned—where I might have said yes, on this occasion I am just too mad at him to do him a favor. And so I say no. This seems fine.

The lesson learned is a reasonable one. My not wishing to take him to the mall is a consequence of his being a lazy jerk. Acting like a lazy jerk *does* make people, me, angry. And when you make people angry, they are not going to feel as disposed to doing you favors as they might otherwise.

But, on the other hand, let us say my teenage child is

regularly lazy and unhelpful. Would I want to institute a more general campaign?

"So long as you continue to act like a lazy jerk around the house, I am not going to do any favors for you."

That is, I will not take him to friends' houses or to skating rinks. I will not give him five dollars for food after the movies. I will not do any of the little extra things that parents do for their children.

That line of action has a very different message than the more simple "I am at this moment too mad at you to feel like taking you to the mall." And I am not sure that it is a message that I want to give.

The underlying question is: What is the role of the parent? Should parents be on the same level as their children or not?

I believe not. Parents need to be above children—protectors, guides, and nurturers. On the one hand, this means that parents are the boss because they are the parents—not because they do not make mistakes. They offer the unconditional deal: I give to you what I feel are the basic rights of any child— which definitely include favors done purely for your benefit. I do this regardless of what you do. Your behavior and what I believe are your basic rights as a child are *not* tied together.

But many parents feel performance and privileges should be tied together. And many professionals in child psychology would, I think, go along with them. If teenagers don't cooperate around the house, then parents should not do any of the extras for them. This is not an unreasonable approach. Nonetheless I prefer the unconditional deal.

What does the unconditional deal teach? Maybe only that there are suckers in the world who can be taken advantage of, treated like dirt, and still they will be nice to you. But maybe it teaches something altogether different. Maybe it teaches that there are ways of relating between humans that transcend the notion that I'll do for you if you'll do for me. Maybe it teaches that out of love and commitment people give to others without guarantees of return. And maybe being on the receiving end of such a deal creates a person who is willing to act the same with others.

In regard to chores around the house, the fact is that if children are expected to do them, and if parents keep after their children to do what they are supposed to, expressing displeasure when they do not, the chores will get done, more or less. But there is no getting around that with the new teenager it can be wearing.

The Consolation Prize

With most teenagers, parents do have to expend much energy in order to produce not all that much teenage labor, but their efforts are not as futile as they may seem. It was always my son Nick's job to bring in the trash barrels from the street when he got home from school on Wednesday afternoons. But without fail when I got home from work on Wednesdays the trash barrels were still out in the street. I would then make him go out and bring them in. And then one day, I believe it was in his junior year in high school, I came home and the trash barrels were not still out in the street. And from that day onward, more or less without exception, Nick did bring in the trash barrels when he got home from school. Why? Had something happened that finally convinced Nick that he should bring in the trash barrels? Or had the repeated lesson finally sunk in by sheer accumulated weight? I think it was neither explanation. Nick had matured, plain and simple. For all those years Nick knew what he should do but just did not feel like doing it. The idea in his budding conscience was just not strong enough to counteract the immediate wants. As Nick matured he finally got to the point where the voice of responsibility did prevail over the need for immediate gratification. And from then on the responsibility always won out. It got to be a habit.

Intrafamilial Hassles

Before going on to issues that extend to the realities of the world, there are still some home issues, though not strictly between parent and teenager, that need discussion.

Sibling Rivalry

Sixteen-year-old Carly to her fourteen-year-old sister Robin:
"Robin, you took my white sweater."
"I did not." (Actually she did.)
"You did too. Don't you lie. I want it back."
"I don't have it. Now get out of my room."
"Robin, you're such a liar."
Instead of leaving, Carly begins to go through her sister's bureau drawers.
"Stop that! Get out of my room!"
Carly ignores her, whereupon Robin tries to pull her sister away from the bureau. Carly, who is bigger and stronger, pushes her away.
"Get the fuck off me!"
Robin picks up a hairbrush and hits her sister rather hard on the back with it.
"Why, you little bitch," says Carly as she turns and punches Robin with all of her strength, hitting her in the stomach and almost knocking the wind out of her. Robin, crying and screaming, runs from the room. Carly runs in pursuit. Their mother,

who was reading in the living room, looks up to see her two daughters rush into the room.

"Carly's crazy. She attacked me. She should be in a hospital."

"I can't stand her, Mom. She takes whatever she wants of my stuff."

"I didn't take anything. She comes in my room, and goes through my drawers, and I can't get her out, and then she hits me in the stomach as hard as she can. I think she injured my intestine. Also she said 'Fuck' at me."

"She hit me with a brush. I swear to God, Mom, one of these days I'm going to kill her unless you do something about her. I mean it, Mom."

"See, Mom, she said she's going to kill me. She's crazy."

"No, you're both wrong," said the girls' mother. "I am going to kill the both of you. Now."

Teenagers are bigger and stronger than they were as young children. Sibling rivalry can take on new levels of violence. Brothers and sisters can and do injure each other. Usually their fights do not go that far, but when they threaten to, parents must intervene. The message must be: "You may not do anything that could cause injury to your sister. And I will do anything to make sure that that does not happen." And parents should not hold back from calling the police if a situation goes beyond what they can handle. The message *must* be that risk of injury will not be allowed.

Yet the general rules for battling siblings remain the same as when they were younger. Other than to separate and banish, parents intervene at their peril.

Brothers and sisters will always fight with each other. It is what they do. Families can have territorial ground rules to cover such issues as phone use, bathroom use, clothes, etc. Such rules are good. But they will not prevent fighting. Nothing will do that.

Parental intervention is always problematic, because as soon as parents enter a sibling battle the nature of that battle totally changes. No matter what the initial issue was, suddenly it becomes a contest for parental favor. The combatants no longer have any interest in resolving the problem. Now all they care about is getting their parent on their side.

"All right. I want each of you to tell me, one at a time, what happened."

This request ranks right up with General Custer's "Come on, let's go to Little Bighorn," as words that guarantee disaster.

"Mom, nothing of mine is safe from her. She takes anything, and she ruins my clothes."

"Once I did. Her stupid scarf. And it wasn't my fault, and she never forgets it."

"Oh? And what about my green pants? And my bead bracelet?"

"You're the liar. The bead bracelet was already broken."

They will go on forever. And not only will a parent's taking on the role of judge promote endless case pleading, but such a role colors the relationship between the two siblings. Older will now usually hate younger, because younger can more usually enlist parent as a protector. It just doesn't work out when parents try to play the role of Solomon in their children's battles with each other. It really is better that they be left alone to work out their own disagreements:

"I'm really not interested in what the problem is. You two are just going to somehow have to work it out on your own."

"But, Mom, that's not fair. You don't understand what she gets away with."

"I really don't want to hear about it."

If parents stay out of the way siblings really can resolve the majority of their disputes, but in their own way and not without squabbling and often not exactly as their parents would have wanted. Assuming there's no threat of physical violence, the absence of parents facilitates this resolution.

Parent Against Parent

Adolescents also can make for trouble between their parents as they readily will play one off the other.

"Mom, could you give me a ride to Beth's house? Her mother can bring me home. I'll be home by nine o'clock. I promise."

"No, Melissa. It's a school night and you have homework to do."

"But, Mom, I just have a little homework and I can do it after I get back."

"No, Melissa. And that's final."

"Mom!"

Thirty minutes later:

"Dexter, where's Melissa? She's been awfully quiet."

"What do you mean? I drove her over to Beth's house half an hour ago."

"You did what?"

"Yeah, she asked me to. She said you had said it was okay but you were too busy to drive her."

"Why, that little shit! I said nothing of the sort. Why didn't you ask me?"

"Why should I? I thought you said it was okay."

"You should have checked with me. You know how sneaky she is. Besides, she's not allowed out on school nights."

"I didn't know that was a rule."

"You don't know anything because you don't pay any attention to anything that's going on with her. You leave everything for me to handle. You just sit here in your chair and watch the news."

"Don't you start in on me, Marion."

"I'll start in what I please."

When teenage children cause trouble, the trouble they cause often does not remain focused just on them.

It is a fact of raising children that parents are not always united. Hence they are ever vulnerable to disagreements arising between them for every problem created by their children. And teenage children often make it more difficult by taking advantage of parental disagreements whenever they can.

In order to cope with this kind of thing parents have to know their own child. If a teenager has bent (or broken) the truth in the past about what one or the other parent said, then it is a good idea for the parents to check with each other.

"Marion, did you say it was okay for Melissa to go over to Beth's house?"

"I certainly did not. What's she been saying?"

But there are situations where it is not always convenient or possible to have each parent check with the other:

"I asked Mom before she left for her meeting if it was okay for me to go over to Beth's house, and she said yes. Could you give me a ride over?"

Conflict

Melissa knows she will be home before her mother's return from her meeting, and is gambling that the visit to Beth's house will not be mentioned by her father.

Often they do get away with this deception, undetected. But what if they are caught after the fact?

"How was your meeting?"

"Pretty good, but Kathleen Teverman certainly can be long-winded. Anything happen here?"

"No. Melissa is back from Beth's and your sister called, but said she would call you in the morning."

"Melissa is back from where?"

At this point Melissa should be confronted with her deviousness.

"You told me that your mother said that it was okay for you to go to Beth's. You lied to me."

Beyond confronting Melissa with her lie and letting her know that they don't like it, there is little more that parents can or should do. Of course, you can more severely reprimand or punish a teenager for deviousness, but you will have virtually no effect whatsoever. For such teenagers the bottom line is *always* whether they think they can get away with it. If in any given instance they believe they can, they'll try, and what happened after they were caught last week will not deter them this week.

Sometimes deviousness works for them. Parents must try to have good communication in order to keep ahead of the game, but that is not always possible. And if children do occasionally succeed in flimflamming their parents, it's no big disaster.

"She tricked us."

"Yeah, I guess she did."

Each Parent in Charge of Their Own Scene

But it is not always adolescent deviousness that pits parent
against parent. They can often disagree all on their own. And
what will always set off a serious battle is the intrusion of one
on a scene already in progress.

> *Sean's mother came into his room:*
> *"Sean, I thought I told you to turn down your stereo."*
> *"I did."*
> *"It's just as loud as it was."*
> *"It isn't. Anyway, this is the way I like it."*
> *"Sean, turn it down."*
> *"But I already did."*
> *"Sean, turn it down, or I'll turn it down."*
> *"Don't you touch my stereo. I bought it with my money."*
> *"Don't you dare tell me what or what not to do."*
> *"You can't touch my stereo."*
> *"You better watch it, Sean!"*
> *Enter Sean's father, who has been in the next room.*
> *"You two are making more noise than his stereo. Elizabeth,
> it's not on that loud. Sean, just keep your door closed."*
> *"The stereo is too loud. I'm handling this."*
> *"You weren't handling it. You were just arguing. You have
> to learn to back off sometimes, Elizabeth. You and Sean always
> end up yelling at each other. It's like two kids."*
> *"Don't you dare contradict me in front of Sean. Don't you
> see what you're doing? You're giving him permission to walk
> all over me. He knows you'll always come in to take his side."*
> *"You're wrong, Elizabeth. You don't know what it's like.
> The two of you always screaming at each other."*

There is a rule. The rule is that once a parent is involved
in disciplining a child, the other parent should stay out of it

—except to back them up, or unless invited to take over. They should never intervene if it is to contradict, even if they totally disagree with what the other parent is doing. To do so is a major mistake.

Intervention that contradicts:

1. Undermines the authority of the first parent. There is no way around it. It says to the child, "Your mother's authority is not absolute. You can count on me stepping in, if I don't like what she is doing," which in turn

2. Does sabotage the son and mother's working things out (just as with siblings), because the son always knows if he can keep the fight going long enough his father will intervene. And

3. Just as with siblings, it creates an unnecessary source of anger—mother toward son. She now has an ongoing grudge against her son, because he can bring his father in on his side against her. Last, and definitely worst of all,

4. It will invariably infuriate the first parent. He or she will feel belittled ("I'm not a good enough parent") and intruded upon ("This is none of his business. It was between Sean and me"). And serious and ongoing hostility can result.

It is to be avoided.

"But isn't it better to prevent something from happening between the two of them? You should see how they go at each other sometimes."

Short of violence, where one should absolutely intervene, if necessary calling the police, intervention will improve nothing. It will only make the intruded-upon parent more angry.

"But there can be real abuse, without its being physical."

This is true. Continuing verbal abuse from parent to child can damage.

"Jamie, you're an asshole. You don't have any fucking sense. You're a loser and you're always going to be a loser."

If the verbal abuse by one spouse is continual, and if attempts to stop it go unheeded, only then does it become appropriate to say something to Jamie. Then a parent does need to say that what the other parent is doing is bad, that it is that parent, not Jamie, who is at fault.

"Your father is wrong to say all that stuff to you. He gets too mad, and he says things he shouldn't say."

Although it is important to say this to children who are the victims of repeated verbal abuse, it must be done with great caution nonetheless. Criticizing another parent does set up an always unfortunate bond—in this instance, mother and son against father. If this is necessary in order to preserve a child's self-respect, then it must happen, but it should never be done lightly.

In matters of child raising, parents like to feel backed up by their spouse. This is very basic to marriages. Husbands and wives want recognition for doing the best they can. They know that they make mistakes. Lots of them. They need support, not criticism. We would all like to point out what we perceive as our partner's mistakes, and what better time than when they are making them. But that just is not our best role. Ours is to support. Even comments delivered later in private often are ill advised.

"I wish you would ease up in dealing with Susan. You should hear yourself sometimes. It really would be better if sometimes you could just let some things go. Even if they bother you."

This sounds reasonable, but the fact is that most parents resent being told how to parent by their spouse. They can read it in an article, hear it on television, even hear it from a counselor, but not from a spouse. (Friends should definitely be wary about criticizing a child-raising practice without being asked. Often it can be wiser to poke cobras with sticks.) Parents can, of course, discuss things after the fact, even criticize each other, but they should be prepared for a battle.

Different Parents, Different Rules

"But we end up with different rules. Ricky and Rachel know that when it's just their father, he's going to say yes to lots of things that I wouldn't. Isn't it important that we be consistent?"

Not really. Parents can never expect that they will react the same in all situations. They cannot communicate about everything and usually one parent is less strict than the other. There is nothing chiseled in stone that says parents must be the same. Children learn early that different rules apply in different situations—at home, at school, alone with friends—and they adapt their behavior to each situation. In the same way they adapt to dealing with their mother and father.

"If I need money I always ask Mom, because with Dad I always get less money and a lecture besides."

This is neither bad nor good. It is reality. What does have to be consistent is that when one given parent is in charge, he or she is the boss and his or her rules apply.

III

Reality and the World Outside

Thus far I have talked of cozy subjects like mouthy ungrateful teenagers, unwashed dishes, and broken curfews. But there is a big world lying in wait out there—real, frightening, and very much a part of the lives of our teenage children. This is the adult world in which they will have to make their way for the rest of their lives—the world that includes sex, drugs, broken relationships and marriages. These and a thousand other hazards bring down adults with regularity; it should be no surprise that they snare a good proportion of the semi-adults we call adolescents.

7

Divorce

Children do not like for their parents to get divorced. But divorces happen anyway. Many divorces. Since 1975, the divorce rate in the United States has held fairly steadily at one divorce for every two marriages (National Center for Health Statistics). Divorces do create problems for children. That is inevitable. Most children learn to cope with divorce, but it is always a problem for them. Are children inevitably scarred by divorce? Opinions vary, but clearly, at the least, divorce is a major disruption in their lives.

"I Want to Worry About Acne, Not This"

"Couldn't they at least have waited until I was out of high school? I don't want to have to deal with this."

There is no good time in the life of a child for his or her parents to divorce. For each age divorce creates its own special problems. Adolescence is the period in which children don't even want to *think* about their parents. They want distance. They also want stability. No major disruptions, please, beyond the battles that the teenager initiates.

Divorce destroys this nirvana.

"Yeah. I want to be able to spend my time worrying about adolescent things like sex and acne and school. And now I can't even deal with that because I keep worrying about Mom and Dad. It sucks."

Children genuinely resent their parents for putting their own adult needs and problems over *theirs*.

"Yeah, she's lived with the guy for seventeen years. What's her big hurry that she can't wait a couple more?"

Having one's parents get divorced is a major loss for teenagers. Teenagers want separation *but on their own terms*. The loss of the safety and security provided by the nuclear family is not what they have in mind.

Moving

A major problem for adolescents, one that does not trouble preteens nearly as much, is that divorce often leads to a change of residence.

"I'm not going to leave my friends. Mom says she can't afford to keep the house now, and she's looking at houses in Ashton, which she says are cheaper. But I'm not moving there. No way. I don't know anybody who goes to Ashton High. And I don't think I'd fit in there so good."

A sudden move can be difficult for a teenager in high school, when friendships are paramount. It will cause deep resentment for even the mature and understanding adolescent. Plans that at least allow the teenager to finish up at his or her old high school are often worth some inconvenience to the parents. But sometimes this accommodation is not possible. And where not, such a move can be hard for teenagers.

While a move may be inevitable, certain other, very negative aspects of divorce are not so inevitable.

It Was My Fault

"If I weren't giving them so much trouble, then I don't think they would have gotten divorced. Most of the time when they were fighting, it had to do with me. I know the divorce was my fault."

Unfortunately, children do quite frequently feel that they have caused their parents' divorce. More often than not, there really is not much real basis for that feeling, but it's there anyway. This misconception can bring on a crushing amount of guilt. For this reason it probably is a good idea for at least one parent to address the subject with their children, even if they haven't said a word about it.

"Evan, do you think it was in any way your fault that your mother and I separated?"

And even if he says, "No," parents should still respond:

"I just wanted you to know that though you have upset us at times, and your mother and I did have fights about you, you are not the reason we separated. That had to do with us. Problems between us had been going on for a long time and had nothing to do with you."

Even explanations as simple as the above really can help. To hear it directly, from the horse's mouth, can allay many concerns. And a parent need not go into great depth either.

"Your mother really began to treat me too much like a child. And over the last couple of years it made me have trouble getting an erection when we had sex. I'm vulnerable to depressive episodes, and your mother would get hostile when I would get depressed."
"Dad! Please!"

They don't want to hear about it. Simple, straightforward, and without a lot of details is all they want or need to hear about the reasons for a separation.

Caught In Between

Probably the most horrible of all divorce situations is for teenagers to feel caught in the middle. The main rule for parents getting a divorce is not to pull their children into the battle, not in any way, shape, or form. Never do it.

"I am not saying this because I want you to think badly of your father. I really mean this. It is only that I want you to get a fair understanding of what went on. I just don't want you to think badly of me. But your father was never an easy man to care about. He can be very cold. You know that. He has this way of making it seem that everything was always my fault. You know how he does the same thing with you and Jeffrey."

"I am not prying. But I do think that I have the right to know if your mother and Tom say anything about me. That is my business."

It may be hard for parents to resist these ploys, but they must. It is simply not fair to children to ask them to take sides. It is not fair to involve them in any adult conflict, much less one between their parents. They cannot handle it. It's bad for them.

As I have stated repeatedly, the main psychological work of adolescence is that teenagers pull away from their parents in order to establish a necessary sense of their own independence. To pull them back into the web of their parents' divorce can destroy that process. Worse still, it can stir up inappropriate feelings toward one parent or the other as parents invite them into an adult complicity, even an intimacy, that is far *too* adult for adolescents to understand and handle. Once these feelings are stirred up they lead only to bad places, and create intolerable conflicts within the teenager.

It may be hard for parents to avoid pulling their children into the divorce, even unintentionally. It can be particularly hard when one parent hears from the children that the *other* parent is not playing by the rules.

"Dad said that one of the reasons that you got divorced was because you had no sense of money, which is also why you keep running short now, not because he does not give enough child support."

This cries out for a response.

"I mean, I do have to set Sammy straight. Am I just supposed to let his father say anything? I know him. He'll convince them that I was the worst bitch in the world and he was a saint."

Blatant untruths deserve simple rebuttals. But beyond that, the great urge to "set the record straight" should be resisted. There is a hidden benefit to this strategy. In time, in the majority of instances, it is the parent who refrained from speaking ill of the other, who did not try to bring children to his or her "side," who comes out looking the best.

"Mom always said all this stuff about Dad, and I never knew what to think. But Dad always stayed out of it. I never liked it when Mom said all that stuff. I guess she had her problems."

When one parent puts his or her own needs (usually, to get back at the divorced spouse) over their children's needs, adolescents are perceptive enough to see the gambit for what it really is. We may not understand, but our children do not really care who was to blame. Remember, adolescents in particular are mainly interested in themselves. Nor is it important that they "know the truth." Only to us is it important, not to them. They just want to know that their parents are okay and that their parents still love them. Maybe someday they will want to know, when they can deal with it as adults, and at a distance. But not now.

We owe it to our children that we not enmesh them in our adult affairs. As much as we can, we want to provide them with a childhood, with an adolescence. This is where they grow best.

Parenting Alone

One in every four children in the United States lives in a single-parent home. In approximately two out of three of these homes, the parents had been married. In the single-parent homes, just over 10 percent of the children live with fathers (U.S. Bureau of the Census).

Raising a child alone is usually a more difficult task than doing it with a partner. In many ways, the difficulties in single-parent homes are more for the parents than for their children.

Certainly it is to a child's advantage to have both parents in the home, but children can adapt to many kinds of living arrangements, and they tend to flourish according to how the parenting is done, rather than whether there are two married parents in the home or not.

Probably the greatest difficulty for the single parent of a teenager is that there is no one to fall back on—not for day-to-day relief during shrieking battles or for support when difficult decisions must be made.

"Rachel, don't you have the least bit of sense in your head? Didn't you realize what you were doing?"

"I'll do whatever I like, and I won't listen to anything you or Dad says."

"I can't deal with her anymore, Edward. You try."

"Just like your mother says, you must not have a brain in your head. Do you know what could happen to you?"

Some single parents are lucky enough to have some kind of burden-sharing arrangement with the other parent who now lives elsewhere but fairly close by. Some live with relatives. But many must do it all on their own.

Though single parents are perfectly capable of raising teenagers, having to parent alone *is* harder. Yet though alone, single parents do not have to be completely alone. They can seek out support. Talking with friends, relatives, the lady behind you in the supermarket who is glancing at the book on adolescence, anybody, really, can be useful. They cannot help with the work, they cannot be there at the moments of decision, but talking with others is virtually a necessity. It is a mistake to be a parent in isolation.

"Edith, it was unbelievable. I'm home thinking that Lisa is at her friend Karen's studying and then she calls and asks me

to pick her up at Megan Rasner's, who I had said she was absolutely not allowed to hang around with. Lisa thinks I say stuff and it doesn't mean anything, so I really let her have it when I picked her up. I don't know what I'm going to do with her."

Edith does not have any solutions but she does fulfill the very important task of making you feel not quite so alone.

Stepparenting

A number of years back I heard about an unusual situation. A man whose wife had died and who had three children married a woman whose husband had died and who also had three children. Suddenly, six children, but despite the odds against them the two families blended amazingly well into one. Of course there were some disagreements, but there was a lot of love and respect in the family, a lot of caring within the family as a whole. Their name was Brady. Their secret, of course, was that they were not real, but only the product of television scriptwriters. Real is usually a little different.

"You're Not My Father"

"You can't tell me what to do, you're not my father."

"It's not just that he won't obey his stepfather. I can't believe how disrespectful he is to him sometimes. And not just Chris, Valerie does it too. Both of them. They actually ignore him, they act like he isn't talking. They are impossibly rude to him."

"Yeah, well, he's an asshole. I don't know why Mom married him. I guess she was lonely.

"And it's not that I compare him to Dad. It's that he really

is an asshole. Even the way he talks. 'Marian, when shall we leave?' What an asshole! It's better that I ignore him instead of punching him in his fucking face.

"And he always has his hands all over her. He's disgusting. He's such a letch. And I can't believe her. She likes it. I feel like I don't know her.

"And you should see how he holds his fork."

"They don't give him a chance. He's really a much nicer man than their father."

"Don't you think you should at least try to get along with him? At least for my sake?"

"See. She always says that. She could have waited to get married. What's her hurry? She sure didn't consult me about whether they should get married."

"That's not true. I asked you about it."

"Sure. What am I supposed to say, 'No, Mom, don't marry him'? She should have known."

And it is not only with stepfathers. Teenagers can be equally nasty to stepmothers.

"You're going to have to obey your stepmother."

"But, Dad, she's a lunatic about picking up. I put something down for a second and she's after me. It wasn't this way before she came in the house. It's not fair to me. I have to change after all these years. I didn't marry her."

Stepparents are not impervious to this abuse by their stepchildren.

"I hate him. He's trying to ruin our marriage and he's doing a very good job."

"Now, Elaine, you have to understand. Timmy's not a bad kid. It is a big change. We're asking him to change a lot, and

maybe it's not reasonable to want him to be quite what you're used to."

"He just wraps you around his little finger. You should hear what he says to me when you're not around. He doesn't do anything and he thinks he can treat me like a maid. I don't think you really know what kind of a child you've raised. He says anything to you and you believe him. Maybe I'm really the intruder. Maybe I should just leave you two alone and go back to Cleveland."

If the children are very young, a new stepparent in the home can, over time, come into the role of a true parent. Some children live from an early age with a mother and a stepfather, but see their natural father with regularity. (Less often, they're living with their natural father and see their mother outside the home.) These children see themselves as having two fathers, usually with a stronger attachment to the stepfather. They do not feel any conflict about having "two fathers." To them it seems natural. In these situations divided-loyalty problems are created by adults.

But if the children are older when the stepparent appears on the scene, more usually they will not view this new adult as a full, true parent. Often they will see the stepparent as an intruder—in a home situation that was set—even as an intruder who perhaps caused or certainly ensures the permanent breakup of the natural parents and who now competes for the attention of the true parent. The many reasons for resenting a stepparent are normal and understandable. Add to that a teenager's normal wish not to do anything, add the knack for making excuses and acting like a sullen lazy jerk, and you have a problem.

"No, seriously, it's not that I'm lazy. She really has no right to tell me what to do."

Many teenage stepchildren, acting like lazy jerks, genuinely believe that they are doing nothing wrong. With a divorce and remarriage, they feel that their parents' original contract with them has been broken and now, in all fairness, they are free to act as they wish. It has always been *their* home. Their stepparent is but an invader on their birthrighted turf—with no right to tell them what to do. Their deal never included a new parent. It was not their choice. They feel shortchanged. They may be right. Yet though it may not be what they wanted, it is what they got. And they must live with it.

Must I Like My Stepson?

The Bradys really were a happy family. Each family member genuinely liked all the others. *Real* stepchildren often genuinely do not like a stepparent, and real stepparents often genuinely do not like their stepchildren, especially when those stepchildren consistently give them a hard time.

"I wanted it to go well. I wanted to be a nice parent. I did try. But I feel so rejected. They treat me like dirt. What did I ever do to deserve this? You know how I really feel about the two of them? I think they're spoiled brats."

Fortunately, it is not necessary for stepparent and stepchild to like each other. It would be nice if it happened, but it does not have to be. What is necessary is that the facts of the situation—a stepchild's obnoxious behavior or a stepparent's difficult personality—must be given recognition by the arbiter, the natural parent.

"I know that Stephen gives you a hard time. I've done all that I can think of to get him to act better, and I know that

it hasn't worked. He is awful to you, and I'm sorry for that. I only hope it doesn't ruin things for you and me."

It is always a mistake to downplay how obnoxious, how disrespectful a stepchild might be. And even though there may be nothing one can do about it, just recognizing how bad it is can go a long way toward making an abused stepparent feel not quite so abused.

Likewise with children and difficult stepparents:

"I know Vivian gets very upset sometimes when you don't clean up after yourself, and I know that you're really not that bad about cleaning up. But that's the way she is. And I do understand that having her be the way she is can get to you sometimes. Nobody says you have to like her. But I do want you to treat her with respect."

One big happy family it is not. But it can work out anyway.

8

School

School performance goes a long way toward shaping an adolescent's future. Many parents view their teenager's report cards as the first true indication of whether they will be successful in life. But parents of teenagers must remember that they serve much like the trainer of a fighter: he can train his man but cannot go into the ring with him. The best you can do is give advice between rounds.

"You have to spend more time on your homework. It's your future that's on the line. You don't want to end up like your uncle Leo, do you?"

"A D? You got a D in your Spanish test? How? I thought you said you studied, that you knew the chapter."

"You have detention all next week? . . . You did what during chorus?"

It can be frustrating. Parents have little direct control over how their teenagers do in school.

Academic Performance

However, parents do have considerable *influence* over their children's school performance. But for the most part, even influence is restricted to the grade-school years. Parents who help their children in school start early. They put time, energy, and caring into school-related activities. They read to and with their children. They show a continuing interest in schoolwork. When there's homework they make sure that their children do it, and make clear that it is a top priority. By their attitude, their interest, and their willingness to participate, they communicate that school is very important.

Eleven-year-olds with a positive attitude toward school and good work habits normally become sixteen-year-olds with a positive attitude toward school and good work habits. Conversely, eleven-year-olds who hate schoolwork and have never been able to sit down and do homework on their own are almost always going to have a rough time in high school. Good high-school students seldom spring newly born from mediocre middle-school students. Children are the product of all that has gone on before. Parents who hope to bring about major changes in an adolescent's high-school performance are quite likely to be disappointed. This does not mean that parents should not try. But they do need to be aware that much has already been established. Of course, maddeningly, previously good students may do poorly in high school. Usually, but not always, this is because they discover and are overwhelmed by the joys of socializing.

What Parents Can Do

A combination of ambition and anxiety is what motivates adolescents to do their schoolwork. The anxiety is very important. (It works well with adults too.) The anxiety is the fear of what will happen if they do not do their schoolwork. Their parents will be angry at them and they want to avoid unnecessary battles. They may lose privileges. However, their main fear is that failure can jeopardize their future. This is a powerful motivator. But some teenagers can completely shut out even this warning siren.

"You really don't worry about your future?"
"I guess once in a while. But no, I don't think about it."

Without anxiety as a regular prod, teenagers drift, force their worries away, and go nowhere.

"But I'm not just going to sit still and watch my kid go down the tubes. There have to be things I can do."

Parents do have options, of course. Those who can afford it send their children to boarding schools with highly structured programs and an environment that promises to shape up their children. I am not a great fan of this solution because I liked living at home during high school and I liked having my children home. But undeniably there are some children who do respond positively to the usually greater structure of boarding schools. Some do not. For parents who cannot afford or do not choose such an option, what remains?

Motivating Your Teenager

There are a number of ways to motivate teenagers to do their schoolwork. One common practice is to use punishment.

"If you do not get all C's or better for this term, we are going to ground you until you do pull up your grades."

Similar motivators include withholding permission to drive, forbidding an upcoming trip, altering plans for a special summer vacation.

Parents also use the promise of reward.

"All B's for the year and we'll buy you a car."

Threats or promises do sometimes work, but more often than not they only work for a while. They rarely solve the problem.

Another common motivating technique is the motivational lecture.

"Two years from now high school is going to be over, and you're going to be on your own. It's up to you what's going to happen. If you do well enough you can go to college, and we will help you with that. But right now, you won't be able to go anywhere. All that you will be qualified for is to work at McDonald's or to bag at a supermarket."

In some homes these lectures are given very frequently—and are then often followed by even shorter, more passionate versions.

"You do nothing. I can't stand watching you. You're gonna be a bum. A bum. A goddamn bum."

Perhaps unfortunately, but these types of intervention usually have little positive effect except that they may help the parent feel better, which is fine. They're not likely to help the student.

Here's the main problem with all these plays: capable children who perform poorly in school do not lack the desire for success. Most of them do want to do well in school.

"Do you want to do better in school?"
"Yeah."
"So why don't you?"
"I don't know. I just never feel like doing the work. I say to myself sometimes that I'm going to start to try in school. But it never gets anywhere, because I never can get myself to do it. I don't know why I can't. I guess I'm just lazy."

I might say that they are motivated but not disciplined. They would like to do better; they just cannot make themselves. The one motivator that might push them along—anxiety about their future—is too successfully pushed away.

Therefore, working on motivation rarely produces results. So what's left?

Supervision

There really is only one form of parental intervention with teenagers that can make a difference: direct supervision of their child's study. There are many ways to do this but it's never easy. One plan can involve a mutually accepted study time with at least one parent in the house and available for supervision. During study time the teenager is not allowed to do anything else. No TV. No phone calls. Nothing except schoolwork. It is not possible to force a child to do schoolwork, but it is fairly possible to enforce a ban on doing anything else.

The study period must always be in force regardless of whether a child has homework or not. This last proviso is necessary because the study-time plan can quickly be defeated:

"I don't have any homework."

"I did it in school."

"I don't know my assignments."

Or the ultimate:

"I left my books in school."

Tough. The study period remains. During the study period the child is not allowed to do anything other than schoolwork. If that means staring into space for an hour, so be it. Parents cannot make a child do homework. But they can usually enforce that during a specified time period their child does nothing else.

It is a good idea to set up a study period of limited and specified duration. When the time is up, the teenager is free to do whatever he or she wants. This plan works best because it says to the student, "If I can just survive until nine o'clock, then no matter what, I'm free."

Study-period students should not be allowed to lock themselves in their room with the door closed. Parents need to check regularly. Sometimes working at a kitchen table, away from the distractions of one's room, can further the cause. Listening to music is not necessarily ruled out. With some children, it can actually help them to stay with their work.

Important to the success of this plan is that *parents* must stay with it. Initial resistance may be fierce and the amount of work done limited. But over time, with parental persistence, some children can begin to stay with a study time. They will not fight it so much. They will like the fact that the work is now getting done, that they are getting fewer hassles from their teachers, and that their grades are going up.

Parents can check regularly to make sure that homework is done. This usually requires the cooperation of the school because the parents will need to know, for example through daily assignment sheets, what the homework is. Some teachers don't mind taking the time required to help in this regard, but others do. Some schools will even supply an in-school counselor or teacher to monitor assignments.

One problem with supervision plans is that a great deal of parental time and effort are required. This is certainly the case when, as often happens, the student in question does not meekly accept the added supervision. Teenagers absolutely hate it. Particularly at first, they will fight it tooth and nail. So supervision can be yet another thoroughly unpleasant task. And parents cannot let up. Just because a student has settled into a regular routine of study does not mean that the pattern will hold when supervision ceases. Almost certainly it will not. Parental supervision should be looked on as a long-term job —two or even three years perhaps.

"But if he is constantly supervised, if he only does his work with us standing over him, how will he ever learn to do it himself? Isn't it a necessary part of independence that they are allowed to fail, and then learning that they can fail, they'll start to work on their own?"

Were it only so. That's what I used to believe. Let high-school students learn by their failures. But it does not work. They learn nothing. They only keep failing.

"But if they go to college, with no parents to stand over them, never having learned to work on their own, won't they just stop working and flunk out?"

Some do. But my argument in favor of the hands-on approach with failing students is that if they can be made to study regularly, over an extended period of time, then it becomes a habit. Having been able to study for significant periods of time, if they then choose to make themselves study, even without the overseer, they are more able to abide their new taskmaster—themselves.

With adolescents who, for whatever reason, cannot make themselves do their schoolwork, more supervision is the only real answer. Unfortunately, even this does not always work. There are some teenagers who resist even the best parental efforts. There are some who, despite all that may be done, continue to fail.

Time as an Ally

Yet even with those who continue to fail despite every effort, all is still not lost. Waiting in the wings, ready to come on in the not too distant future, is one last, very powerful force: true independence. Shortly, they will be on their own and they know it. The anxiety they have held at bay these many years will finally catch up to them. And maybe they will have matured enough to be ready for it.

"I know I totally screwed up high school. I just fucked around the whole time. But now I guess I have to get my act together. I don't have a choice. Either I start getting serious and work at something, or I'm going to screw up my whole life. I really will end up a bum."

Many former high-school screw-ups do go to college. Many do well. Many perfectly successful adults were disasters in high school. They did get their act together. On their own. When they had to.

What should parents do with teenage children who do badly in school and could do much better? If parents wish to put in the effort, if they are willing to put up with considerable unpleasantness, they can actively supervise their children's schoolwork at home. And this may help. But it may not. If not, their only recourse is to wait and to hope that with time, with maturity, with anxiety about the future looming not on the horizon but directly overhead, their children will at last be willing and able to work.

Troublemakers in School

Academic performance is usually of first concern for most parents, but misbehavior in school can be an accompanying and sometimes especially trying problem.

"Hello, Mrs. Shepardson, this is the high school. We are calling just to check to make sure that you knew that Clarence was not in school today."

"He wasn't?"

"This is just a routine call to let you know that Clarence was not in school today. Thank you."

Click.

"Hello, Mr. Tellman, this is the vice-principal from the high school calling. Did you get our note saying that Mary Ellen was suspended for three days? She cannot come back to school until this Friday. At that time she will have to be accompanied by a parent."

"Mrs. Windle, this is Marge Gladner from the high school. We just wanted you to know that Jason did not show up for his detentions for the last two days, and since he has to serve two for every one detention missed, he will have to serve four days' detention.

These situations seem to demand a parental response.

"Clarence, you cut school today. You're grounded for two weeks."

"Jason, you've been skipping detentions. Well, you can skip going out this weekend."

Yet I am not certain that such responses are necessary or even desirable. How much do parents want to get involved with behavior problems that take place in a realm that already has a system for behavior control? I think not a whole lot. One such system at a time is probably enough. Parents should confront their children. They should certainly voice their displeasure.

"I got a call today from your school. They said you have not been showing up for detention. I do not know what your problem is, and I really don't care. But you had better start serving those detentions. I do not want to get any more calls from the school."

Beyond that, involvement may be counterproductive. Parents may ultimately be better off letting their teenage children deal on their own with the consequences of their behavior in the outside world.

Parents should also be wary of listening too well to their children's side of the story.

"Dad, it's just like I've been saying. Mr. Farragut doesn't like me. I don't know why, but it's always me who's the one who gets in trouble. I swear to God, other kids are doing more stuff than me and aren't getting in any trouble. He's really picking on me, Dad."

Parents may be tempted to intervene with the school, but they do so at their peril. It is far better simply to say, "I don't know what the problem is. Maybe Mr. Farragut is being unfair. But you're sixteen years old and you're going to have to figure out whatever it is you have to do to stay out of trouble. You're going to have to deal with it on your own."

It's the same issue yet again: as they get older we have to let go. They are no longer answerable just to us. They become answerable to their school, to their employers, to the police, even to the government. Gradually, responsibility for their actions must and does leave our hands.

"Ronnie, I just got a call from the IRS. They say that you filed fraudulent tax returns for the past three years. Well, mister, you can just forget about going out on weekends for the next month."

"But, Dad, Roselyn and I had planned to take the kids to the circus next weekend."

"Well, mister, you should have thought about that when you filed those fraudulent tax returns."

"Aw, Dad."

9

Sex

Michael and Yvonne

"How old are you?"

"Fifteen."

"Do you have a boyfriend?"

"Yeah. His name is Michael. Do you want to see a picture of him?"

"No, thanks. How old is Michael?"

"He's sixteen."

"How long have you been going out with him?"

"This Thursday is going to be our four-month anniversary."

"Do you love Michael?"

"Yeah, I love him a lot."

"Does he love you?"

"Yes. And he tells me he does. He's not afraid to say it."

"Do you and he have sex?"

"Yeah."

"How often?"

"Maybe two, three times a week."

"How do you get to do it that much?"

"Well, sometimes we meet after school at my house, when my parents aren't home, and sometimes he sneaks me up to his room at night. Once we almost got caught when his mother came in and I had to hide in his closet. I really did. And sometimes on weekends, but I have to be in by eleven o'clock, and my parents are usually home."

"Do you like having sex?"

"Yeah, of course I do."

"Have you ever had an orgasm?"

"I'm not sure."

"Why do you and Michael have sex as much as you do?"

"We like to."

"Whose idea is it usually?"

"His. But I don't mind, really. I like to do it."

"Do you use any kind of contraception?"

"Sometimes."

"What do you mean, sometimes?"

"Well, sometimes Michael uses a rubber."

"Why not always?"

"Well, he doesn't like to use them. Sometimes he pulls out of me when he comes. And I know when I have my period, so I know when it's safe. But sometimes I guess we do take chances."

"Don't you worry about AIDS?"

"No, not really."

"Have you ever thought of contraception for yourself?"

"Yeah. But I can't really talk to my parents. They'd have a shit fit if they knew I was having sex with Michael."

"What if you got pregnant?"

"I don't know. I don't like to think about it. But I guess I'd have the baby. I wouldn't want to have an abortion. I think I would keep the baby."

"What would Michael do?"

"I'm not that stupid. I know he probably wouldn't want to get married. Besides, we're too young. But he would always be the baby's father. I told you, we're in love."

"You're Michael, right?"

"Yeah."

"What do you think about Yvonne?"

"I love her."

"You don't just say that to her so that she'll have sex with you?"

"No, I love her. When we first started having sex, I used to say I loved her and I probably didn't mean it. I knew she wouldn't do it unless I said it. But I do love her now."

"Do you like having sex with her?"

"Yeah, of course I do. Do you think I'm gay?"

"Do you think Yvonne likes it?"

"Yeah. I think she does. She says she does."

"Does she have orgasms?"

"I don't know. I suppose so. I don't know."

"She said that sometimes when you have sex you don't use a contraceptive."

"Yeah. I don't really like using rubbers. I mean, I do most of the time 'cause I don't want to get her pregnant. But sometimes I just don't feel like it, or I forget and don't have any rubbers."

"Yvonne doesn't say anything?"

"No."

"You're not afraid she'll get pregnant?"

"I don't know. I know we should be more careful. But no, I don't really worry about it."

"What if she got pregnant?"

"I don't know. I don't want a kid. I know Yvonne wouldn't get an abortion. She's said so. I don't know what I'd do."

"Would you get married?"

"No. I don't know. I don't want to get married. I'm too young. I don't really think about it."

Michael and Yvonne are perhaps not a typical teenage couple. They are more sexually active than most and perhaps less mature. But there are many adolescents who are that sexually active and who are no more mature in their thinking about what they are doing. Not only are they having sex, but they do not see a problem with it. While many do worry about pregnancy, sexually transmitted diseases, and parents' disapproval, the majority of teenagers simply do not consider it wrong for people their age to have sex.

The New Age of Sex

The new teenager *does* have sex earlier. The same cultural changes that have given birth to the more outspoken teenager have inaugurated a major change in attitudes about sex. People talk about sex much more openly. Sex between single men and women is not only widely accepted but is done with a casualness that was unthinkable forty years ago. Teenagers are just part of the trend: they have sex earlier, and more casually as well.

From all that I have ever heard teenagers say, they definitely now feel that sex is a normal part of their lives, and that they have a right to have it—if they so choose. This is a big change from when I was in high school.

There has especially been a change for girls. Sexual activities that would have previously branded a girl a "slut" are now okay in the eyes of her peers. The social pressures against sex for girls have dropped sharply. The increase in working mothers has also affected teenage sexual activity. Currently both parents work in half of all married families with children (U.S. Bureau of the Census). Teenagers now have more unsupervised time at home.

The net result is that teenagers in the United States are more sexually active earlier than in prior generations.

Should Teenagers Have Sex?

Should teenagers have sex? Is it bad that they do it so young? In some ways these are not useful questions because they are beside the point. Parents know many reasons why sex isn't a good idea for their teenage children. Many believe deeply that teenage sex is just plain wrong. But teenagers have sex anyway, and many have no discernible problems in their lives because of it. Many even have a good time.

"I don't know what your problem is. Me and my boyfriend have been having sex for a year. We do it a lot. We're real careful about protection. I like it. He doesn't take advantage of me. We love each other, but we're probably not going to get married. Neither of us wants to get married until we're a lot older. But we have a real nice time having sex. Not only that, I think my relationship with him is more mature than with anybody else in my life. And the sex is part of it.

"To tell you the truth, I feel better about myself now than I think I ever did before. And I think I understand more about

what a relationship is. I feel now like I'm going to do better later on when I get into other serious relationships, or even when I get married.

"If you don't like my having sex, that's your problem. It certainly isn't mine."

Maybe there really are some teenagers for whom having sex is thoroughly enjoyable and for whom it is a wholly positive experience in their lives. But this is an idea parents have a hard time swallowing.

Problems of Teenage Sex

Problems do come up when teenagers have sex. Pregnancy and sexually transmitted diseases (especially AIDS), obviously, but also a subtle emotional problem.

Sex and Intimacy

To have sex with somebody is very intimate. Sex carries with it great emotional power. This is true enough for adults. With teenagers, sex, in and of itself, can cause them to "fall in love." Perhaps surprisingly, and I have no explanations, most of the more seriously brokenhearted teenagers I have seen over the years have been boys. After their fairly long sexual relationships have broken up, these boys become very upset and cannot pull themselves out of it. Some have serious thoughts of suicide. Obviously girls too can suffer from such breakups. There is no question that sex itself can create emotional involvements that are beyond the emotional capacity of the participants. Of course, this is true with some adults too.

And then there's the converse, which really is not much better, particularly with boys. They will engage in sex but are not even close to possessing any real empathy for the girls. And so they must feign caring about the girl and they are aware of the deception. Clearly, this syndrome breeds callousness. These teenagers are unable to combine sex and emotional intimacy because they are too immature to sustain the intimacy. So they end up exploiting their sex partners; they cannot do otherwise. This sets up a bad pattern for further relationships with women.

Sex in the Time of AIDS

AIDS has dramatically changed the potential consequences of sexual activity. Sex with anybody who has had other sexual partners besides oneself carries with it, for the first time since the discovery of penicillin, the risk of contracting a *deadly* disease.

So far the AIDS epidemic has not hit the teenage population to nearly the extent that it has older age groups. But since AIDS symptoms usually take a number of years to show up in the infected, it is possible that AIDS has spread into the teenage population without yet being apparent. The risk for teenagers is definitely there, and many teenagers *are* more wary of multiple sexual contacts, or of having sex at all, but the effect of AIDS on their sexual behavior overall is unclear. What is certain is that there continues to be an absolute need for AIDS education for teenagers.

What Can Parents Do?

The parents' main role in the question of sex is education, but most of that should have already taken place by the time their children become adolescents. By then children should know about the changes that will take place in their bodies and in the bodies of the opposite sex. They should know about the process of reproduction. They should know about the sex act itself and they should know that it will be pleasurable, not just functional. Children may not even be that interested in all this information prior to adolescence, but they should have it nonetheless. The fewer surprises in store for them in adolescence, the better. Also, once adolescence strikes, parents are less useful as an information source. Teenagers want to hear lots about sex, but not from their parents. That is too uncomfortable.

"Well, Larry, I think that it's time that you and I had a little talk about sex."
"Sure, Dad, but I know it all. Listen, I've got to go."

But he probably does not know it all. He would be interested in more information—just not from his father.

One source of sex information available to all teenagers is friends. Unfortunately, this may be a case of the blind leading the blind. Most schools provide some form of sex education, particularly in light of AIDS.

That information can be rather limited. Parents do well to make sure that their teenage children do have access to full and accurate information about sex. Books about sex written for teenagers can be particularly useful. Though the teenagers may show nothing but scorn, such books rarely go unread. Sometimes family doctors can be asked and will talk to adolescents about issues of sexuality where parents are unable to. But if parents feel that there are certain things about sex that they truly want their children to know, the only way they can be certain that this information gets to their children is to tell them themselves.

Much debated is the question of supplying information about contraception to teenagers, or even the contraceptives themselves. Does talking about contraception give teenagers the tacit approval of authorities, including parents? Does supplying them with contraceptives make it more likely they will have sex, with or without those contraceptives?

Were there no AIDS, I would still strongly prefer that teenagers be given information about contraception and easy access to contraceptives. I do not believe these actions tell teenagers that sex is or is not okay. I think providing information tells teenagers that their parents recognize they cannot control teenage sexual behavior, and if teenagers are going to have sex, they certainly should use precautions.

Because of AIDS, I now believe adolescents *must* be supplied with certain very explicit information about sex and about contraception. And they *must* be supplied with easy access to condoms.

AIDS can be spread from having sex relations with another person. Once the AIDS virus gets in a person's body it lies dormant for one to ten years before symptoms begin to appear. Then, usually within a couple of years, the person dies. Always. There is no cure. Someday there may be a vaccine against AIDS. Someday there may be a cure for AIDS. At this point in time AIDS is a 100 percent fatal disease which can be spread by sexual contact. For children to contract AIDS because of a lack of information they did not get because we adults did not want to give it to them—this is not acceptable.

Beyond Education

Many parents may not be satisfied with simply making sure that their teenagers know the basic facts about sex. They may want to convey more than just facts.

"Sex outside of marriage is wrong."

"You should only have sex once you are in a true love relationship."

"You may be afraid that if you do not have sex with a boy, then he won't go out with you anymore. But do you want a boy who really only wants to go out with you for the sex?"

Parents want to protect their children from hurt and disappointment. And usually they prefer that their children, especially their girls, not have sex at all.

Although we know teenagers do not like to hear from their parents about much of anything, including sex, we are their parents and we do have every right to let them know exactly what we think.

Controlling Your Teenager's Sexual Behavior

Parents, of course, often want more than the role of information and opinion giver. They want control.

"What's wrong with that? Theresa is fifteen. I don't want her having sex with boys. She's too young. And besides, I think it's wrong."

They can even try to enforce sexual behavior—or the lack thereof.

"I won't let her go out on dates until she is sixteen."

"I won't let her be at home in the afternoons when there is no adult there."

"If she does go out, I will keep close track of exactly where she is and who she's with."

To some extent such supervision probably does make a difference. But in today's world teenagers do have the freedom and the opportunity to have sex if they really want to, and they are not above sneaking out of their house in the middle of the night to get it. Parents delude themselves if they believe otherwise.

10

Drugs and Drinking

From earliest recorded time the species *Homo sapiens* has known about the countless substances occurring naturally in the environment which, when ingested or injected or smoked or inhaled, can change moods or states of consciousness. In the last few decades scientists have multiplied this number with seemingly countless *unnatural* substances and bizarre derivatives from natural ones.

Mankind has known about and manufactured all these potions for the simple reason that day-to-day living can be hard. Life can be stressful. It can be anything but fun, and some of the changes that can be induced chemically can be just the opposite—quite pleasurable indeed. Many substances have the power to remove the effects of stress. Adults consume alcohol and caffeine and tranquilizers and cocaine and various other drugs in great quantities.

Small wonder, then, that adolescents just entering into adulthood, beset with all the anxieties I have been discussing in this book, seem to have a craving for mind- and mood-altering chemicals. In addition, teenagers by definition like to experiment with new things. They do not like the word "no." They do not like to listen to the advice of adults.

It is therefore inevitable that many, if not most, teenagers are going to drink or use drugs. And because many, if not all, of these substances are to some degree physiologically or emotionally addictive and potentially harmful, so too will many teenagers have substance-abuse problems.

Drugs in America—Two Problems

Today in America there are two separate teenage drug problems, one of them devastating, the other not nearly so catastrophic. The first involves the inner-city poor and two drugs, heroin and, especially, crack (a concentrated, smokable form of cocaine). The second problem involves most of the rest of the teenagers in this country who indulge in a variety of drugs but not, for the most part, heroin and crack.

Among the poor in the inner cities, the use of crack has become epidemic. It is a swiftly addicting drug, much more so than the powder form of cocaine. And it has the power, once the addiction is set, to take a life and so totally dominate it that all else falls away. It also can be a very nasty drug. When not on a high (and these are very brief with crack), addicts are vulnerable to extreme irritability and depression. It is also a horrendous drug for teenagers. Because of the enormous number of addicts there can be a great deal of money to be made, very quickly, by those involved in the selling of crack. This leads to an ever-present need to recruit young drug dealers. More often than not, these kids end up as addicts themselves. But set against the strong financial incentives to go into dealing, five dollars an hour at McDonald's just cannot compete. Young dealers exert strong pressures on their peers to start using crack. The net result of the crack epidemic is that it is destroying the futures of a significant segment of our population.

In these pages I will mainly speak of the second, and I believe much less critical, problem. The crack scourge of our inner cities is a problem of a scope and origin beyond the range of this book. The other teenage drug problem (setting aside the issue of alcohol for a moment) is the use of marijuana and, to a lesser extent, LSD and powder cocaine among suburban and rural teenagers. There *is* much drug use in almost all our high schools. How many teenagers outside of the inner cities are having their lives ruined by drugs, and how many of these would not have had serious problems anyway? Some. A scourge among adolescents drugs are *not*. They are not destroying our youth outside of the inner cities. Excluding crack, drug use by high-school children is actually down over the last decade, according to the University of Michigan Institute of Social Research.

Still, for many teenagers, just as for many adults, drugs and alcohol *are* part of their fun. Over 85 percent of teenagers have used alcohol before the end of high school. Over 35 percent have used some illegal drug. But most of these teenagers do not have serious drinking or drug problems. Most will continue the substance use into their adult years, and for most it will not dominate their lives. They will be able to handle it.

"Why do they have to drink or use drugs in order to have a good time?"

For the same reason many of the rest of us do, and because the alcohol and the drugs are available. Despite a minimum drinking age ranging from eighteen to twenty-one, access to alcohol for most teenagers is surprisingly easy.

"It's never a problem. Rick's older brother Kevin has a fake ID and he'll always buy for us. Also there are two stores where usually they sell to anybody. And if we're really desperate one of us hangs around outside Mel's Liquors and asks people going in if they'll buy for us. Somebody always will. It's just not a problem."

Access to drugs, at least marijuana, usually presents little problem either. Most high-school students (and many before high school) know somebody in their school who deals drugs, or they know somebody who knows somebody. Some high schools have used aggressive programs to keep drugs out of their school, and in some cases this has affected drug availability, and so drug use. But for the most part the drugs are there. Whether we like it or not, parents have very little direct control over whether our children will or will not drink or use drugs.

"I will tell you exactly what I do. I do not drink or do any drugs during the week—except maybe if there's a half day of classes and we go over to somebody's house in the afternoon and maybe get high on marijuana. On the weekends I go out on both Friday and Saturday nights, if I can. I don't always drink, but if there's a party, I usually do. If somebody there has marijuana, sometimes I'll smoke that. But I don't like marijuana all that much. I'd rather drink.

"I know that when I drink or smoke pot nothing bad is going to happen. I know what I'm doing. I admit I do get drunk sometimes, but I would never drive then, and I don't get rowdy or get into fights.

"I'm not an alcoholic, unless everybody who drinks is an alcoholic, and I'm certainly not a drug addict. I know kids who maybe do drink too much, but I don't drink anything like they

do. And there are a couple of real druggies in our school, and certainly I'm nothing like them.

"But my parents would not understand any of this. What they wouldn't understand is that I'm not a wild kid. I drink and sometimes I smoke pot. I do it to have fun, but I know what I'm doing. I'm never in any danger.

"You know what I like best? I like to party, hang out with friends, and either drink or smoke some pot. My parents would have to prove to me that I'm different from other kids, that what I'm doing really is a problem. And I don't think they can."

The Influence of Parents

Children see themselves as experts. They do not accept that their parents might know as much as they do, and they totally deny that their parents might know anything at all about what's best for them in their own teenage lives.

Parents want to give adolescents freedom but also keep them free from harm. Teenagers also want freedom from harm but it's not such a high priority with them. Teenagers are more willing to take risks. With their adolescent sense of invulnerability they genuinely believe nothing disastrous could happen to them.

"That's right. I'm willing to trust Jennifer. She can make the right decisions about almost everything. But not about drugs, or drinking. I know what they can do. She doesn't. She thinks she knows. She thinks she knows about everything. But I can remember how naïve I was at her age. And it genuinely scares me to think of her out there, on her own, dealing with things that can really harm her, and her just not having the sophistication or maturity to protect herself."

"I knew my mother was going to say that. She thinks that I don't know anything."

It would seem that adolescents only listen to themselves. Yet parents do have influence on whether or not their children drink or use drugs. However, as with most issues of adolescence, much of that influence was brought to bear prior to the teenage years.

Children who have confidence in themselves are more likely to avoid drinking or drug problems. Families with a strong code of ethics (whether religiously based or not) can influence their children's substance use. Children who are raised in strictly religious homes are much less vulnerable to influences outside the family, and can have much lower substance use. Examples of this phenomenon would be Hasidic Jews or the Amish, or any group of people newly arrived in the United States who live together in closely knit communities in their new country.

But even in families whose day-to-day life is not guided by the rules of a particular faith there can be other kinds of faith and ethics that can make a difference. We now enter a somewhat fuzzy area. People often speak of "family values" or "moral standards" as buzzwords for what we used to have in this society but do not have anymore. I'm not going to get into this debate, because it's not my subject, but there is no question that some teenagers have, while others do not, a sense that there is more to their life than the strictly day-to-day. Perhaps this quality could best be described as a sense of purpose.

Maybe this purpose is simply to be successful, to make a lot of money. Maybe it is to excel at sports or at academics or maybe at both. Maybe the purpose is simply to try to do well in one's life, to be a good person. Every human being probably has a purpose for life different from that of everyone else, and as long as these are positive purposes of the kind just identified they can provide a teenager with the idea that life must be more than simply feeling as "good" as you can all the time. The truth is that the hallucinogen LSD has been used in a quest for meaning and for experiencing life as fully as possible. It has even been used by really rather genuinely spiritual young people as part of this quest.

But most drug use cannot claim these high aspirations. Most are of the "feel good" variety. Feeling good, or at least okay, is certainly an important part of one's life, but life should be more than that. Those adolescents who do understand this, and internalize it, will place less importance on their alcohol and drug use. They can say yes or no without much problem either way. There is no question that teenagers who do feel more of an overall purpose and direction in their lives are much less vulnerable to drug abuse than their peers who are wandering. And certainly many such adolescents obtained this sense of purpose mainly from their life at home, inculcated in hundreds of different ways during the course of childhood.

"You don't want to be like us, poor, always worrying about money."

"You have talent, Jason, you have a chance to be really good."

But even where parents do not point their children toward specific goals, children can internalize a sense that there is more to life than fun right now. Parents who are themselves guided in their day-to-day lives by solid principles (not necessarily formally religious ones) or priorities communicate this "discipline" almost automatically to their children.

Whether parents like it or not, what they preach to their

children is of little influence compared to what they themselves are like and how they act toward their children. Lectures to adolescents about drug abuse come too late in the day. Much more important is the parental influence all through childhood that has produced, or failed to produce, a sense of purpose in the adolescent. That said, there does still remain for parents an important role in resolving their teenager's confrontation with alcohol and drugs.

What Should Parents Do?

First, parents must decide where they stand. Are they absolutely against any drinking or drug use? Many parents, right or wrong, do not mind if their children, especially their sons, drink. (Many do seem to have a double standard about daughters and drinking.) Some parents do not genuinely mind if their children occasionally smoke marijuana. Parents must decide where they want to draw the line. That line should not necessarily be drawn at what they do not want, but at what they are willing to live with. Between what they are willing to live with and what they absolutely do not want—where they feel their children would be at serious risk.

Drawing the line does *not* give permission for anything less, but rather declares that anything more is out of bounds and dangerous.

Once parents have decided where they stand, what can they do? One possibility is enforcement. With increased surveillance parents can actually try to enforce their substance-use policy. Increased parental surveillance *can* make it harder for teenagers to get access to and to use alcohol and drugs. However, total supervision is virtually impossible and parents' ability to actually control their teenagers' substance use is limited. Some communities have supported greater substance surveillance in schools, and this apparently has caused some decrease in substance use in some places.

Beyond actual enforcement there remains one other option, and its exercise can have significant influence. Parents can talk to their children. After they decide where they want to draw the line, they should give good and clear reasons for their policy.

"We do not want you to drink or use any drugs, ever. You may think that you know what you can handle, but you're wrong. Once you start, without your even being aware that it is happening, they can pull you in deeper and deeper. You may think that you can control them, but in the end, they will control you."

"We do not want you to smoke marijuana, but we recognize that marijuana is not as dangerous as many other drugs that are out there. Pills of any kind, cocaine, and especially crack, are all very dangerous. Those drugs really scare us. We do not want you to ever use them."

Their children may not agree with parental policy, but that is not a problem.

"Mom, you don't know anything. LSD is no big deal."
"I think it is, and I think it is dangerous."
"You're wrong. The worst that can happen is that you have a bad trip. Kids take it all the time."
"I think it is dangerous and kids grossly underestimate its risks, and I do not want you to even try it. Despite what you may hear, it is dangerous. I do not want you to use it."

If parents feel strongly about their children drinking or taking drugs, they should put all their influence on the line. They should say what they think. This does not mean that their children will heed their words, but they may.

Dealing with Reality

One cautionary note about talking to teenagers about drugs or drinking: be wary of preaching a harsher, scarier anti-substance line than the true dangers warrant. You risk a credibility gap. Teenagers are very fast to turn off adults when they feel they are being preached at, rather than talked to. If teenagers feel, rightly or wrongly, that warnings are being overstated, they will lose trust and will reject the whole package. If you want to talk to teenagers—a difficult enough task to begin with— you must make sure that what you say is believable. The best way to ensure this is to be totally honest. Particularly in regard to drinking and drugs, teenagers *do* have a source of information separate from the adult world. This is the "street wisdom" of their peers, and it's not to be scoffed at. It can be wrong, but at times its information can be more accurate than the adult view. On this as with every other issue of adolescence, if what parents say is too out of line with prevailing teenage wisdom it is simply not going to be believed.

Drinking and Driving

Parental intervention *can* make a significant difference in regard to drinking and driving. Therefore all parents should address this question bluntly. No parent should tolerate it. But in order to deliver the message effectively they must get their priorities straight. Parents have only so much influence. They might do well to invest it in the question of drinking and driving, rather than in lectures about drinking in general: "I don't want you to drink. But above all I don't want you to come to harm. Please don't drink and drive, and don't be in a car with anyone who does."

This warning should then be repeated *throughout* their teen-age years.

"Don't worry. I won't drink and drive and I won't be with anybody who does."
"I do worry."

In regard to drinking and driving it is also a good idea to have a special rule about being stranded:

"If you are stranded and the only ride you can get is with someone who has been drinking, or if you've been drinking, call us. Call us and we will come and get you. We will ask no questions. You will not get into any trouble. Even if calling means that you are caught in a lie, being in a different place than you said you would be or a place you're not supposed to be. Call us and we will get you. No questions asked."

But if a parent says this, he must really mean it. The rule sends two excellent messages:

1. The parents place their child's safety over everything else, and
2. They feel drinking and driving is so dangerous that they are ready to abandon all other considerations to avoid it.

Some teenagers will still drink and drive. So do many adults. But it is important that you communicate your feeling that drinking and driving is in a special category of dangerousness—all in all, the most dangerous threat to the safety of the basic teenager. Here parents can make a difference.

It's Against the Law

Another source of possible intervention is already in place, and parents don't have to do a thing. Underage drinking is illegal. Kids get arrested for doing it. Public drunkenness is illegal. Driving with open containers of alcohol is illegal. Driving while intoxicated is illegal. Drug use is illegal.

"Get caught by the police using drugs or drinking and you can be prosecuted under the law. If you choose to drink or use drugs, what you do is not just between you and us. It is also between you and the law. That is out of our control. We can bail you out of jail, but we can't bail you out of a conviction in a courtroom. If you get caught, you will be answerable to them. And there you will have to take your chances."

Substance-Abuse Problems

What should parents do if they suspect that their child does have a substance-abuse problem? Perhaps the first rule is that if parents, correctly or not, think that their child has a substance-abuse problem, they should not ignore it. They need to confront their child.

"Doug, I think you have a drug problem. I think you are high most of the time. I don't think you have control of it. I think that you need help."
"Fuck you! Get out of my life."

It doesn't matter how they respond. The point is that the parents are not ignoring the situation, hoping it will somehow just go away. Parents do not want to make it too easy for their child to continue what he or she is doing.

They should also talk to someone who knows more about

these problems than they probably do. Many checklists purport to tell the parent what to look for as indications of substance abuse, and most of it's pretty obvious: sudden and sustained irritability, oversleeping, decline in school attendance and grades, and so on. I believe parents should *not* try to diagnose or deal with a problem all on their own. I am very wary of parents diagnosing whether their child has a drug or drinking problem. It is very hard to do. Parents and their children can use all the help they can get. Substance-abuse problems can be very difficult to deal with, and such problems can go on over a long period of time. They are serious business, not a "stage" that can be relied on to fade away as the teenager matures.

Sometimes teenagers need hospitalization. Professionals can assess whether this is necessary and they can help to find a suitable facility.

Of course, any plan of treatment ultimately requires the teenager's active and willing participation. Some can be forced to enter treatment programs, usually after they have tangled with the law, but none will change unless they buy into the treatment. What happens when a teenager with a substance-abuse problem absolutely refuses to do anything about it? His parents are faced with a very difficult decision about whether to allow their child to live at home. Some do and some do not. I would not advise parents one way or the other, except to say that when the teenager's problem is destroying the home (literally as well as emotionally, in some cases, because he or she may steal everything of value), parents must look to their own survival. Sometimes all that parents can do is to try to make sure that their lives are not also destroyed.

11

Suicide

Before talking about teenage suicide it is useful to first look at the statistics on suicide for all ages. They are somewhat surprising, and tell us a lot about the nature of suicide itself. On the following page is a chart which shows the suicide rate for men and women in different age groups in the United States.

For my purposes, these are the salient facts:

1. Approximately three times as many men will kill themselves as women. With teenagers this gender ratio is closer to four to one.
2. After age fifty the suicide rate for men keeps going up with age. Men aged seventy-five and over have by far the highest rate.
3. The suicide rate for women drops gradually from age fifty—exactly the opposite of the pattern for men.
4. The suicide rate for teenagers is less than the suicide rate for adults.
5. Suicide by preadolescent children is extremely rare.

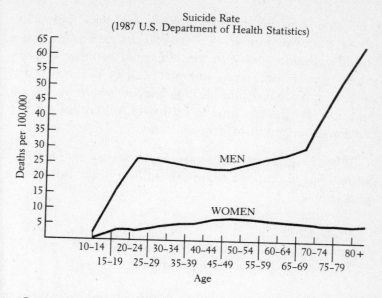

Suicide Rate
(1987 U.S. Department of Health Statistics)

One more statistic, not shown in the chart: the teenage suicide rate, although still lower than for adults, has tripled over the last thirty years, while the overall suicide rate has gone up only slightly.

Why has there been such an increase in teenage suicide? I believe it's because teenagers today face the full range of "adult" problems at earlier ages than they used to. In a more complicated world with, in many cases, less family support, teenagers feel themselves to be more on their own. This is nobody's "fault." It is a different world.

Perhaps of all suicide statistics, the most significant one is the one most taken for granted. It points clearly, if indirectly, to the nature of adolescence: prior to adolescence, with the rarest exception, children do not kill themselves. The idea and fact of killing oneself starts only in adolescence. Why?

When a child is absolutely miserable, no matter how miserable he is, he can still look to adults for solace. No matter what the source of misery, children always see nurturing as a possible solution. But with the adolescent mandate, the absolute turning away from just that kind of nurturing, that solution is no longer possible. Adolescents are on their own. And now, for the first time in their lives, misery and terrible situations can appear to have no solution.

> *"When I was a little kid, I guess I always knew that if things got real bad, I could go cry in my mother's arms. But I can't do that now."*
> *"Why not?"*
> *"I just can't."*
> *"Even if you felt so bad that you wanted to kill yourself?"*
> *"I just can't. It's not there anymore."*

Boys Versus Girls

Why do four times as many adolescent boys as girls kill themselves? The main reason is probably rather simple, and rather grim. It is the choice of method. Girls attempting suicide will most often take an overdose of pills. Probably the second most common method is wrist cutting. Both of these methods are usually not fatal. Boys also use these methods but they are more likely to employ more lethal means. Boys will shoot themselves, hang themselves, or try to poison themselves with carbon monoxide (car exhaust). Unfortunately, these three methods very often work.

Another and very different kind of reason may also be partly responsible for this difference. Since, as we have seen, teenage boys tend to isolate themselves from their parents, they feel they have to keep their problems to themselves. They must work things out on their own. If they cannot, they have few remaining options. Girls, because they at least keep *some* kind of contact with their parents, do have them to lean on in the worst times.

Suicide Attempts

Many more teenagers try to kill themselves than succeed. Statistics on attempts are not very reliable, but girls probably make more attempts than boys. When a teenager attempts to kill himself or herself and does not succeed, did he or she really want to die or was their action a cry for help, or merely a misguided way of getting attention? I prefer to take all suicide attempts seriously. Did they really want to die? Who knows? Did the teenagers who succeeded in killing themselves *really* want to die? A suicide attempt is desperate regardless of what was behind it. All suicide attempts are serious.

Why Do Teenagers Try to Kill Themselves?

Teenagers try to kill themselves for pretty much the same reasons as do adults. They may have been very depressed for a long time. They may have been rejected by a lover. They may feel under such pressure that they simply "can't go on anymore." There are many reasons. But there is at least one characteristic of many teenage suicide attempts that is different from those of adults. More suicide attempts by teenagers are "of the moment," in reaction to a specific and immediate situation to which they see no solution.

Depression and Suicide

Teenagers can *also* suffer from serious depression. By depression I mean an ongoing condition wherein a teenager feels "down," unhappy, has difficulty in generating enthusiasm about anything at all, lacks energy. Depression may be in reaction to a real life situation—for example, a parent's death—or it may not seem to stem from any particular external cause. Some depressions are now believed to have mainly biochemical causes. Also depression can be a concomitant of drug or alcohol abuse.

Depression over a sustained period of time, from whatever cause, can lead to suicide attempts. Teenagers in these situations often do respond to counseling, and sometimes to antidepressant medication. But many have emotional conditions that stay with them through and past adolescence. Their suicide attempts may not end after adolescence.

They Can't See Tomorrow

The following are some reasons why teenagers have tried to kill themselves:

1. In a rage after a big fight with parents that started over something trivial, a household chore left undone.
2. After a breakup with a girlfriend or boyfriend (probably the single most frequent cause of teenage suicide attempts).
3. After receiving a bad report card, when parents had said this report had better be an improvement "or else."
4. School starts tomorrow, following summer or Christmas vacation (the anxiety for some can be overwhelming).
5. After getting in trouble for crashing the car (and not necessarily seriously), being arrested (again, perhaps on a minor charge).
6. When unable to decide whether they should live with their father or mother after a divorce (as an adolescent, it will be their decision if both parents want them).

Common to all these situations is the particular teenage phenomenon discussed earlier, the conviction that there is no tomorrow. Teenagers can feel trapped in situations to which they see no solution, and from which they see no escape. They look at tomorrow and it seems just too awful. These suicide attempts are a teenager's lack of perspective taken literally to its limits. In many cases all they have to do is wait a little while. But this they do not yet know.

Intervention

The good news about teenage suicide is that this is one instance in which intervention can make a big difference, one instance in which teenagers are often eager to hand over the responsibility for their problems to someone else, at least temporarily. Involvement by almost any adult lets a teenager exit safely from a situation they feel they cannot deal with. They may have to deal with it later but the crisis is relieved for now.

With potentially suicidal teenagers, friends can be significantly less useful than adults. Yet not infrequently friends find themselves saddled with a terrible secret.

"Please, Kristin, you have to swear to God that you won't tell anybody how I feel. I'm just telling you because you're my best friend and I need somebody to talk to."

Yet the Kristins of the world are often not enough help. They do not have enough of a perspective either. The burden for them is too great. It is always preferable for teenagers to tell some adult if they know a friend is having really serious problems, even if, as in Kristin's case here, she would be betraying a promise. The burden of keeping a friend alive is an awfully big burden. The adult world really can do a better job.

What to Do

If a parent has any worry at all that her child may be thinking about killing himself or herself, she should ask directly.

"Roger, do you think about killing yourself?"

Parents are often very reluctant to ask such a question because they fear that in asking they may somehow create a possibility that did not exist before. They fear the question may put the idea into their child's head: "I wasn't until now. But now that you bring it up, Mom, it seems like a very good idea."

"Can you promise me that if I ask him about suicide, the question won't put the idea in his head? Can you promise me that he might not, later on, try to kill himself?"

There are never guarantees, but certainly the risks of *not* asking a troubled teenager are far greater than the risks of asking. The teenager may be lying when denying the thought, but at least you have asked. At least he knows that you know something is wrong. He knows the line of communication is always open.

"Well, I just wanted to ask, because I worry. But if you ever do think about killing yourself, or harming yourself, before you do anything, talk to me or your father first. Okay?"

If They Say "Yes"

"Yeah, sometimes."

If adolescents admit to thinking about killing themselves, this is not necessarily a disaster. Many do. But the admission should always be taken seriously. The first point to determine is if there is an immediate danger. If the child admits he is seriously thinking about suicide in the near future, it is time to get immediate help. This means calling the family doctor or a mental health professional, if the parents know one. Many communities have twenty-four-hour crisis services. Or parents can call the emergency room of a local hospital, or they can call the police. Parents need to talk to someone experienced in dealing with potentially suicidal teenagers. Often it may be useful to have the child talk with a professional as soon as possible to determine whether hospitalization is necessary. If not, do the parents need to keep a twenty-four-hour watch on their child?

These are steps that rarely need to be taken. But just knowing that one is ready to take these steps, if necessary, can make the whole suicide less, not more, scary. The goal with any teenager who does talk about the possibility of suicide is to get him into counseling, even if the situation is not critical. This is one area where counseling really can make a difference.

Warning Signs

As discussed, teenagers try to kill themselves for many different reasons. But where is the line between nonsuicidal misery and potentially suicidal misery? How can a parent tell? Beyond certain very definite warning signs I will discuss shortly, I don't think it's possible to be certain. Adolescence is often an unhappy experience. Being thoroughly miserable is not uncommon with normal teenagers, and this can be for all sorts of obscure and highly personal reasons. When should parents start to be concerned? Probably the best answer is: when the misery continues. When a teenager does not seem to have ups and downs, but mainly just downs, and when this pattern continues, not for a week or two, but for many weeks, a month, two months.

This is when parents might do well to consult a mental health professional who has experience with teenagers. This professional will want to visit with the teenager. The parents can then ask: Should they be worried? Is there anything they can do to help? Would it be helpful if the adolescent talked regularly with a counselor?

The Mandatory Warning Sign

The one warning sign that must not be ignored is when teenagers talk about wanting to die. Not all such talk means that a teenager is contemplating suicide, but most teenagers who do try to kill themselves talk about it first, perhaps in a letter left lying around, or in a school essay reported to parents by a concerned teacher, or simply in things said at home.

"I don't know. Life really is shit. Really, what's the point?"

"You and Dad care so much about my grades. Maybe if I do bad enough this marking period, I'll just kill myself. That'll get you off my back. Won't it?"

"Maybe everybody would be happier if I just wasn't here anymore."

Such remarks should not be ignored. Parents should ask directly whether the teenager really feels like killing himself. As discussed earlier, appropriate steps should be taken, depending on the response. There are no guarantees, but if parents are aware of their children and willing to be a bit

intrusive when they believe it's warranted, they can head off
many potential tragedies.

"You're sure you don't want to kill yourself?"
*"No, Mom. Please. I promise. I'll tell you if I'm planning
to do it."*

The End of Adolescence

"Is this you, Harris?"

"What do you mean, Mom? Why?"

"But you're nice."

"Yeah. What's so strange about that?"

"But it's been so long since you've been nice. Do you see what you are doing right now?"

"Yeah, I'm helping you clear the supper dishes. What's the big deal?"

"But at the end of the meal you just got up and started clearing dishes. I didn't ask you to do it, or anything. And you've been very pleasant about it, as if you want to help me."

"Yeah, well, I do. Why should you have to clear the dishes? You made the meal, and you have had a busy day. It's the least I can do. I like it when you take it easy."

"But do you hear yourself? Do you hear what you're saying? You haven't said anything like that since you were eleven. All

*these years, this is exactly how I wanted you to act, and now,
suddenly, you're doing it. I don't understand."*

*"I don't know. I guess I was kind of a jerk. Well, I guess
more than 'kind of.' But now I'm older. I'm not a kid anymore.
I know how hard you and Dad work. And a lot of it is to help
me. I love you, you know."*

"My, darling."

Harris's mother dissolves in a puddle of tears.

"Hi, Sheila."

"Hi, Dad. How was work?"

"What?"

*"How was work? Anything special happen today? You know,
any interesting clients or anything?"*

"What?"

"Why do you keep saying 'What'?"

For, again, they have changed. And almost always the
change is for the better, and often for the *much* better. They
are friendly. Cooperative. Willing to take out the trash. The
girls no longer disagree with everything you say, nor do they
criticize you constantly. The boys talk pleasantly and even, if
that is their nature, a lot. Moreover, they genuinely seem to
like you. They show it, they might even say it—with no
embarrassment.

Not all teenagers change in this way, but most do. What's
going on? Time. Mainly just time. Nature has spoken at last.
The needs of the baby self are no longer so great. They are
genuinely able to behave in a more responsible, less self-
centered manner. The more mature version of the self that
for years had been on display only away from home can now
be seen in the kitchen as well, at least some of the time.

The adolescent mandate to strive for independence has finally *achieved* the goal. The teenagers are on their own and

they seem to be able to survive. They *are* independent. They really do not need their parents anymore. Their parents are no longer a threat. It is possible to have warm feelings toward them, to care about them, because these feelings are no longer a challenge to their sense of independence. The sexuality of adolescent boys, previously unfocused and all over the place, is now satisfactorily under control, focused quite keenly on favorite females outside of the home, clearing the way for affectionate feelings toward the mother that will not be sexually tinged. They are nice. They like you. They can be in the same room as you.

Remember: It's a Stage

It is very important for parents to understand that adolescence does have an end, that teenagers do change. When parents are going through their children's adolescence they need to know they are witnessing a *stage*. Granted, some children continue right through their adult lives being irresponsible, self-centered, needing always to be nurtured, never truly establishing their own independence. But parents can be fairly certain that *their* child will change automatically, and for the better. This knowledge can make the bad parts seem not quite so desperate. Even the immature teenagers who turn out to be a continuing burden to their parents tend to grow more pleasant in their demands. The unabated nastiness does run its course and fade away.

"*I hate you and I hate Daddy and I'm not going back to school, and I don't care what you do to me.*"

"You're sure that she's going to change? You promise me? Is it possible to get something to that effect in writing?"

Ultimately, much of being the parent of a teenager is a

matter of faith—that adolescence *is* a stage—particularly the adolescence of one's own child. Dealing with the new teenager can be pretty rough. At such times it is necessary to know that, awful as they may seem, the end product is going to look so much better.

Yet this *is* so. Not only that, but of all the parental interventions, admonitions, and advice that seem so fruitlessly to bounce off one's child, some do get through. Parents' efforts during the teenage years not only do have an impact; they are often crucial. But sometimes this is a little hard to see.